Together we love the Earth

By Loving Each Other

Global Religious Science Ministries

Young Soul Planet

Duality is the Illusion

REV. LORANA CLARK

BALBOA
PRESS
A DIVISION OF HAY HOUSE

Balboa Press books may be ordered through booksellers or by contacting:

Balboa Press
A Division of Hay House
1663 Liberty Drive
Bloomington, IN 47403
www.balboapress.com
1 (877) 407-4847

Printed in the United States of America.

ISBN: 978-1-4525-5912-4 (sc)
ISBN: 978-1-4525-5911-7 (e)

Balboa Press rev. date: 02/21/2014

DEDICATION

*I am dedicating this book to my friend and confidante,
who did not hang around on the Earth plane long enough
to see me complete it. Lynn this is for you; I love you...*

Thank you

A Gigantic thank you goes to my good friends Jonathan and Maaja for all their help editing. Thank you to Dee Pacheco for her proof reading. Huge thanks to my heart, my daughter-- Miss Nadine for your help and encouragement. Also thanks go to Ann Maid for her literary advice and Jan Elliot for her continuing inspiration.

COVER DESIGN

Designed by author and illustrated by Delights Fantasy Art

www.Delightsfantasyart.etsy.com

Authors note;

The information in this book is totally based on my own experiences, visions, and journey... it does not solely reflect the views of any organization other than my own.

Contents

DECLARATION

- You are a unified field of light energy

- Localized in a physical body

- Manifesting the essence of God

- Within the Density of matter.

How's that for a description of the totality of you and me --and every other Being --whether they know it or not?

Those who don't know it usually don't show it.

Those who see God as *outside* of themselves live in superstition and fear.

I am Spirit, I am Eternal...And I Create.

Infinite Spirit is what I AM, and right now I am using the creative power of mind to create my personal world. I have learned how to harness the power of my Intention to create what I choose to have in my life. Through the studies of Metaphysics via Science of Mind, Astrology, Channeling, Buddhism, Mysticism, and other Spiritual and healing modalities, I have come to learn some *great* truths--and some *not so great* truths. I am alive in my mind/body... I chose this lifetime from some deeper or higher level so I plan to make the most of it. Perhaps I can help you do so as well.

These things I believe;

- I believe in a creative force that I am a part of.

- I believe that it directly responds to me if I align myself with it.

- I believe in what is called God.

- I believe that within God all things are possible.

- I believe that on this planet we play in a land of duality, and are totally convinced that it is real.

FORWARD

The official start of the New Age of Aquarius was on Dec. 21, 2012, but the effects began earlier, and will continue well into the 21st century. Everyone will be impacted by the new energy. This book is for anyone who would like to explore the many possibilities that have been bandied around about the coming New Age. This work is a sometimes humorous, yet practical approach to the problems facing our human condition and especially for those wrestling with addictions. It is a primer for anyone who is just beginning to ask questions about Spirituality or exploring Spirituality as a means of healing their life. This is not a dry dissertation about the *shoulds and oughts* of life. It explores the possible origins of our humanity with a "now what" attitude and relates it to our current age as a species. I look at many of the problems facing our societies, especially the addictive disorders that seem to affect us all in one way or another. I will share with you some of the things you can do to help yourself. By helping yourself you help all of us, because we are all ONE human family. This book will help you find your way out of destructive patterns and into healthy living and loving.

I believe that this time on Earth is very special. You have chosen to be here at this time in human evolution. Therefore, you have a real chance to "Wake Up and Smell the Coffee".

You don't have to be lost in addictions to realize that things have to change. We have to come together as one human family if we are going to survive the next century. If you don't do anything else to prepare for the transformation and change that appears to be taking place on this planet; do just this......
DO NOT BUY INTO FEAR....Duality is the Illusion in the 3D (dimensional) reality that we find ourselves. Fear is one of the names of duality and joy is the other. Put your currency into the Joy Bank. It will help everyone.

There are many theories about what will happen in the New Age. I am attempting to help you understand the general flavor of them. You are urged to research any of these subjects that catch your valuable attention. I believe there is possibility in all of them, but they are not necessarily all going to happen. Perhaps nothing of great significance will happen on any one day, but it is undeniable that change is in the air. It may come gradually, and one day we will all be living in a different world. Great change has already happened with the age of computers. In less than 100 years we have gone from a primitive to an advanced culture. When my mother was a child, she rode to town in a sleigh pulled by a team of horses. When I was born, hardly anyone had a TV. It is also possible that a catastrophic event could happen in one day that will change our world forever. Whether major Earth changes happen or not, we need to find our way out of the mess we have created for ourselves, and this planet.

I toyed with the idea of titling this book, The Rednecks Guide to Enlightenment, because I want it to speak to average people in simple vocabulary. I decided against it, because it was perceived as a joke book. I offer a practical approach to finding a way out of chaos. I will also take a hard look at the dogma that keeps us living in fear. By sharing my unique stories, dreams, visions and training, I can help light the way into the New Age. Duality is the Illusion here in 3 dimensional reality, and there are no rights without wrongs. We can walk on this Earth without fear by summoning our innate wisdom and courage to go in Peace.

I have been blessed by Spirit to have witnessed many unusual and extraordinary events in my life. In times long past, I might have been called a Prophet, a Seer, a Healer, a Mystic or a Witch. I have studied many schools of thought over my 60+ years. I've combined into this work many of the things that I have read, heard, and experienced, regarding the New Age. I am not attempting to sell any particular doctrine. I'm sharing many of my conclusions after years of studying the normal and the paranormal world. I will also share some of the tools you can use to create a better life experience for yourself. By putting ideas into simple terms, I hope to open doors in your mind to a Spiritual path that will help you. I invite you to pursue any path toward your enlightenment that suits you. Find one that interests you, and let it show you the light within your heart… ***All paths have Heart***; what resonates to you will be a perfect place to start

INTRODUCTION

Welcome to the New Aquarian Age....

We are in a time when the indigenous people, visionaries and prophets of this planet, either now or in the past, have counseled us that something big is going to happen. Our biblical literature tells of an end time. Almost everyone is feeling that something will happen.

If we talk to economists, they say that we are in danger of global financial collapse. If we talk to fundamentalists, they tell us that God is returning to Earth to collect the best of us. If we talk to UFO enthusiasts, they will tell us that the space brothers are coming to either get us, save us, or destroy us. If we talk to environmentalist, they will tell us that we are destroying the Earth and are doomed. If we talk to a geologist, they will tell us that we have had many Earth changes in the distant past, and we are approaching a pole shift and another ice age. If you talk to a psychic, you will hear of our Ascension.

There are many highly educated authors who have written of upcoming possibilities. Then, there are those who guffaw it all, and say nothing is going to happen. I have listened to them, and I have also studied Science of Mind for many years. I am absolutely positive that some kind of shift will take place, because of the cosmic law of Attraction. This is a law as dependable as the law of gravity, which tells us that *what we think about, we bring about.* With so many people thinking about the Mayan Calendar and the end times, something has to be brought into manifestation… What will manifest will depend, at least in part, on the *predominance of thought,* coming from all the people of the world. We need all minds to focus on the positive and with so many people experiencing some form of addiction, it is paramount to heal this dreadful mental disease and free their minds of negativity. Ironically the only way out of addiction is by taking a spiritual leap and claiming the God energy within, to bring about healing.

We are coming into the New World Age of Aquarius. I would like to point out that Aquarius is the sign of brotherhood, but it is ruled by the planet Uranus. Uranus is dubbed the destroyer and rebuilder. Some things may have to be torn down before they can be rebuilt with love and brotherhood.

Information has been slowly leaking into the mainstream media about past contacts with space beings. Perhaps people from different planets have also faced the crisis' we face now and will be able to help us. The possibilities are almost limitless regarding Alien influences. The brotherhood of Man could extend to other beings and other worlds. Are we ready? As citizens of Earth, we could soon realize that we are also, **Citizens of the Universe.**

Who are WE? & what is REALITY Really?

CHAPTER 1

Duality is the Illusion

I heard the voice of Spirit speak loudly in my head. It seemed to me, to have come from a loud speaker. I was in my kitchen making dinner, when a booming voice stated that "**duality is the illusion**". It sounded so loud that the neighbors should have been able to hear it. At the time, a booming voice in my empty kitchen didn't seem 'all that strange', because it was not the first highly unusual incident of this type in my life. I learned later that a booming voice is one of the hallmarks of Archangel Michael. I have been blessed to experience his presence many times in my life, especially when I've needed strength or pertinent information. At that time, I did not really understand where this bit of information fit into my life. I now realize that the pronouncement was the focus of my Spiritual quest. I understand that duality is the illusion that allows us to have choices. If we don't know what we don't want; we can't define what we do want. There is no light, without darkness. There is no right, without wrong. Both are necessary for us to be aware that we exist in the denseness of 3d (dimensional) reality.

I believe we are all part of God, and we are made of God-stuff. I use the word God here as a descriptive term for 'All that Is'. I don't believe it is possible to be separate from God, but it is very possible to believe that you are, and in that way, to *separate yourself* from God. I am not talking about some guy in the sky with a clipboard, keeping score of our actions. I believe that we are the keeper of our own clipboard and we are judging ourselves. Sadly we are usually much more apt to give ourselves a bad report than a good one. In the land of 3d reality everything has to be shades of either good or bad, because of the duality of existence.

The idea of God and the devil, is a wonderful example of "duality is the illusion"; good vs. evil, devil or angel, saint or sinner. I don't believe in a being called Devil. I do believe there are devilish and ignorant souls, on both sides of the veil of birth and death, who operate out of fear and lack. I can only thank them for my opportunity to cultivate compassion through them.

To be lost in addiction and have it controlling your life and happiness is the closest thing to a devil I have ever witnessed. Realizing **who** you really are, which is a spiritual being; having a human experience, helps you to step consciously into your God nature. Once you do so, you can then obliterate the devil of addiction or any other negative condition that has control of your life. In the land of duality, darkness cannot live where there is light. Our society has been in darkness for many years but, the light is slowly seeping into the crevasses of darkness and en"light"enment will soon take over. I believe that enlightenment is a process that every soul is seeking and not reserved for a few Gurus on mountaintops chanting OM.

If God is *"All that IS"*, there cannot be anything outside of God. Therefore, a Devil must be inside God. God created the duality we live and learn in. We have named the negative side of duality the devil and imagined that it is outside of "All that IS". The idea of a Devil has gone viral within the matrix of human consciousness. There are those who totally believe in a Devil, and for them the Devil is real. The idea of "devil" is also very important to organized religion, because they must have something to fight against, in order to save us from it. The Devil is the original scapegoat. The Devil made me do it, is a convenient excuse for bad behavior. Within the creator, we are free to play in any area of duality we choose.

The philosophy of Science of Mind states that if we believe something long enough, and with emotion, conviction, and intent--we can literally think it into being. Therefore, the idea of a Devil, believed in over and over with the emotion of fear, has created one in the collective consciousness. The collective consciousness is the predominant thought pattern of a family, a nation, or the entire Earth. You are free to experience devils and demons if you choose to. We must have free-will to be able to choose life experiences, which will help us learn and grow. There is no doubt that demonic energy exists, because we keep recreating it with our belief in it.

In the oneness of all life, everything, every being, every star system, must ultimately originate from the same ONE thing. There could not be two things first. It is the old question--which came first, the chicken or the egg? *The egg came first, fertilized itself, and had twins.* No matter how far you reach out with your mind, you have to come to the conclusion that everything, be it Humans, Aliens, or Galaxies--everything had to start with one first cause. Since there could be nothing before, or outside of, this first cause, what is created has to reside within it.

In the land of duality, we hear that the high road is peace and love, and the low road is war and hate. If duality is truly illusion, <u>we can't take either side</u>. Too much of anything creates imbalance, and chaos is the outcome. It has been reported by people who channel spiritual information, that the beings from the Pleiades went all the way to the side of peace, love and unity, which led to stagnation in their world. I am not saying this is true or false, but the concept is sound. If there were no aggression, what would get done? HUMMMMMMMMM would be the nature of reality and there would be no incentive for change and growth. However, if there were only aggression, what would get done? All energy would go to the war effort, and life would become unmanageable.

We recreate the illusion of duality every day, in every way, and love doing it... or hate doing it... but we do it nonetheless. You always find yourself on one side or the other of the polarity of life; *until you don't.* Enlightenment is what we are all seeking but, it is not a sudden event, after which you can walk on water. It is having the internal lights on, and stepping on the path toward total awareness of whom and what we really are. The difference between an awakened life and one still asleep, is that one understands duality and accepts it, learning from it; and the other feels like a victim of it. Spiritual teachers all over the globe, teach nonresistance to both sides of duality. What is, *Is*, and acceptance is the key to awareness and balance. The Spiritual master is sitting in meditation, keeping the world in balance. The Spiritual master realizes that duality is an illusion.

Chapter 2

Naming and Claiming

It seems to boil down to one concept: in the land of duality there are only two choices, joy or suffering. You can't consider one without the other. Perhaps, our purpose here on Earth, is to add to the collective bank of one or the other of these choices. If this is true, which one would you choose? Which one are you choosing right now? Perhaps, our purpose is to recognize both sides, and choose neither. On an individual level, everyone would say that they would choose joy over suffering, but that doesn't appear to be the truth. If duality is illusion, then it follows that it is the separation between its two sides that causes suffering, and the integration of the two that will bring us peace, and ultimately joy. An Enlightened Master accepts everything that happens around him as *'what is'* and does not let his spirit get hooked into either side of duality. On a young soul planet such as this one, there are not very many Enlightened Masters but, I believe their numbers are growing. A question to ponder is this: if we are free to choose, why would anyone choose suffering? (*The answer will be very enlightening*)

Humans need to assign a good or bad value to everything in the land of duality. We do this first by naming. We have self-awareness by naming. "I think therefore, I AM. I have just named myself *I*. I AM is the name of our GodSelf, which is the God within us. We are beings that are conscious of ourselves. Our conscious mind needs to set us apart so that we can perceive the created universe that we reside in. Duality is necessary to distinguish ourselves from the table we are sitting at. In the book of Genesis, we are told that Adam was given dominion over the animals, and could name them. To me that means, he was setting himself apart from them by calling them different names. After we name something, we can conceptualize it. Our neuron-synapses have a place to go when we think of something that we have labeled. The road toward enlightenment consists of remembering that we are the awareness that uses the names, not one of the things named. I have a body, not I am a body, is the proper way to understand self.

Science now knows that at the deepest level everything is vibration. Sound is base vibration and therefore; words are the first manifestation in form. We can't know how God created the diverse universe but we can use the knowledge that creativity exists and that we are part of it. When we name something we are labeling its vibration. Perhaps, being made in the image and likeness of God is referring to our ability to create things and attract circumstances in our life. When we name something we apply our creative power to it. Our words are much more important than we are aware of, especially when you consider the idea that words are vibrations and vibration is everything. What we say, and what labels we put on ourselves and others has more power than we might have thought.

We are using our creative God-given energy to create what we name. When the people we see as authority, such as our parents, label us a certain way we accept it without question. *When we get older we can use a therapist to rename ourselves.* When we label ourselves as poor, sick or broken, that is what we attract to ourselves. The old axe "the rich get richer and the poor get poorer" is true because that is what they have named themselves deep in there consciousness. The rich expect riches and the poor expect nothing. What we expect deep in our consciousness is what we attract. (More about the law of attraction later in the book).

It is apparent that we are creative beings, and one of the ways we do so is by naming and claiming all the stuff we create. Some force in the universe, that we are an intricate part of, packs dense the molecules to become a chair. It is our job, as humans, to name it, and agree collectively, that it is a chair. Then we must distinguish my chair from your chair, which can create the conflict of ownership. Duality is ever-present in conflicts because there must be a right and a wrong. You can begin to change your life by naming things differently. Instead of experiencing so many judgments about what is right or wrong, I recommend calling something *'interesting'*, instead of good or bad. If something is interesting it captures your attention, it has your awareness, and from that you can choose whether or not you would like to give energy to it.

Often addictive behaviors are turned to when we have named ourselves as bad or we have adopted that name from someone else. The root of addictive behavior is often trying to cover up or run from the names we have adopted for ourselves. Addiction is no longer just one person's struggle with darkness; it has become a social disease. To help cure the disease of addiction it is important to name addicts as humans with an illness, rather than weak or evil people. If we continually name ourselves as victims of our physical body, we will not have space in our consciousness for health. If we hold the consciousness of health in our mind, we are much more likely to experience good health. No matter what you are struggling with, it is very important not to get hooked by the names you place on situations or each other. *I might be experiencing a condition in body, but I am a Soul.*

CHAPTER 3

Voices of Wisdom

B esides the booming voice in my kitchen, I've received information intuitively for most of my life. By getting in touch with your psychic or inner self, you are able to use that energy to live a happier more productive life. Your intuitive energy is available to help you make choices that will promote happiness and joy on your journey through the land of duality. Everyone is intuitive in some way. As the new era comes in, I believe that intuitive information will become more prominent and valued. Many of the children that are born now are much more open to extrasensory perception than children used to be. It is also true that paranormal experiences are not being shamed or suppressed as much as they were 50 years ago.

This is not a book about Channeling but, I would like to share the flavor of what was given to me in Channel so many years ago. Channeling is accomplished by moving over in your mind and letting the energy of a master teacher or guide speak through you. It is not 'being taken over' by another Spirit. It is more like lending your voice box to a wise teacher. First and foremost you must understand that Intuition, Inspiration, and Imagination are all God in Action. I use these mental tools all the time. I like to think of these tools as God's voice inside of me. When we put all three channels of God's voice in action, we can create our life in abundance and joy.

Usually, channeled information brings forth wisdom about the planet and the Spiritual nature of life. You have to be really careful, and extremely centered in your own being, to do extensive psychic work, such as channeling. If you are not careful, you can mistake valuable energy for the less aware energy that is residing in the astral plane. The astral plane is where our thought forms seem to take on a life of their own. Perhaps, you have heard of people on drug "trips" who were hallucinating very negative or very positive events. I am reasonably sure that their mind slipped its physical boundaries, lost the constraints of time, and experienced the astral plane where the content of mind was revealed to them. Since your subconscious mind stores everything you have ever said, done, or witnessed, the crime scene on TV with all its blood and gore can present itself to you while you're hallucinating. The astral plane is like a storehouse for all thought and intention. I equate it to the field of infinite possibilities. The Astral plane is a level up from our current awareness and is where discarnate beings are contacted. I call the spirits residing there "dead Uncle Fred". The mental plane is said to be "above" the astral plane and is where Ascended Masters reside. Angels are on still higher planes. When I channel information, I do so from the mental plane. No one really knows for sure what lies beyond our physical world, but many have reported visiting other realms. Higher or lower appear to be labels we use to wrap our understanding around these concepts. It is here in the land of duality that we need to assign order to our thoughts about concepts such as planes of existence. Try not to get lost in the actual hierarchy of Spiritual or Angelic realms. What is; IS, but where it is only helps us conceptualize Spirituality.

In the astral plane, fearful energy can coagulate into some pretty unpleasant experiences. If you would like to receive information from the Spirit world you do not have to learn to channel. It is entirely possible to simply ask for your own inner wisdom to come in one of the three forms available to everyone. They are the same three voices of God I spoke of earlier: Intuition, Inspiration, and Imagination.

Does it make sense that a God, who created the entire Universe—the Earth, the stars, and the galaxies, would expect us to rely on the voice of other created beings to hear what s/he wanted us to know? Some glorious souls claim to have the corner on the market of God's voice. Surely, many people do hear the voice of God, but sadly, some have an agenda of power and control. The biblical prophets were channeling a voice they called "God". I believe most of the wisdom they brought forth was sound, no matter what brand of "God" they were associated with. I believe we can all hear the voice of "God", if we stop and listen with our natural tools. We do not have to depend on anyone else to do it for us. We must believe that we can, keep our ego in check, and then understand that we are not just crazy when we get inspired wisdom. You must listen with your heart as well as your mind. The gifts from the creator are as close as your breath.

As children we are taught that our imagination is child's play, and not real. On the other hand, creative visualization uses imagination to bring what we desire into our life. Imagination is a natural, God-given tool that we can use to create our life experiences. In truth, we do just that, all the time but most of us are not aware of it. I have heard so many people who have received valuable intuitive information worry that, it is "just their imagination" and therefore of no value. This could not be further from the truth.

Simon Peter and WE

I channeled a being called Simon Peter, or St. Simone, depending on what he felt like calling himself on any particular day, and a group-soul that only referred to itself as, "WE". I received some very interesting information about the origins of humanity, and how to love and honor each other as immortal souls, from these energy beings.

Simon Peter teaches of our Oneness with all life. He often states that we are our own judges and juries. We are far harder on ourselves than our conception of God would ever be. The energy that came through me, called simply "We", seemed to be coming from beings from another planet. Their message was that everything is going along as planned, and we need not fear. While channeling "We", I have often been heard to say that, *"We have seeded this planet"* or, *"this is a young soul planet"*. I am sure, in the depths of my being, that these statements are truth. I firmly believe that we are indeed, spawned from the people of the Stars. We are StarSeeds with an untapped potential that we are now, hopefully, beginning to realize. Science says we have twelve strands of DNA, of which we only use two... Perhaps 2 is the age of the human race's collective self.

CHAPTER 4

Young Souls

*E*verywhere in biblical literature, we are told that we are "Children of God". We are advised to be, "as little children". God is our Father, and Mary is our mother. The idea of this being a young soul planet easily fits into what most of us in Western culture have already been taught. The Bible is calling us children, and young souls.

What is expected of young souls? Can young souls be destructive? We most certainly can be. We can destroy our air and our water on this planet, and perish in our own ignorance. Our own infants will touch a hot surface, or step off into air and fall, until experience teaches them differently. As young souls of the universe, our mother, nurturer, and keeper Gaia has been tolerating our growing pains, much as a parent will forgive a child the mess it creates. We are growing up and it is time for us to go to the school of the cosmos, and leave our safe haven. Our playpen no longer can sustain our actions because we have grown big enough to tear down the sides.

There is a phenomenon called the hundred monkey scenario that helps to describe how we are spreading the ideas that will awaken us to a higher sense of who we are. It was observed that monkeys on an isolated island would pick up a particular trait and pass it on to the monkeys on other islands even though there could be no physical contact between them. What seemed to be happening was that when enough monkeys caught on to an idea it spread telepathically. Like the hundred monkey scenario, if enough of us within the "We", become aware of the larger picture of our objectives, and place in the universe, it will tip the scales, and all will become aware of a new paradigm, a new truth, a new age…If we don't, our species could die off, and another, perhaps not quite so aggressive species will be brought forward, and the process will begin anew. Perhaps this process will begin anew anyway. Just as everything you can experience is cyclical here on Earth, so too might be the process of giving a place on this beautiful planet for souls to mature.

To fail at the project and not advance, would seem to be a vast waste of energy. In reality there is no wasted energy, as energy can change from one form to another, but never goes away. The work of en-souling another species would simply begin again. Science is now beginning to understand that time is only relevant to us here on Earth, and there is no time as we know it in the galaxy. With that understanding, our perspective of time wasted or lost, is of no value or consequence.

Saying that it is a young soul planet might not set well with the New Age crowd. Everybody wants to be an "old soul", which is no different than being a kid and wishing and wanting to be grown-up. Once we are grown-ups, we wish we could be a kid again. I was in a workshop once where the instructor asked everyone who thought they were old souls to raise their hand. Then he called everyone with their hand in the air slow learners. Back then, my ego wanted to be an "old soul". Now I just want to be a peaceful soul and pass my classes. It doesn't matter what grade we are actually in. Baby, young, mature, or old soul; we are all still on the path to enlightenment. It is the nature of duality to compare ourselves as young or old. The older we get the more awareness we gather. To put this in perspective, passing kindergarten is important, but getting out of high school is a major event.

Environmentalists tell us, that we are polluting the planet and causing global warming. They believe that the planet that we live on will have to perish, because of us. It is doubtful that this will happen. The planet may very well shift and change. We may not be able to sustain life as we know it here, but the planet will continue to exist. "The Earth Will Abide". Our goal is to do the best we can to mature and awaken to our higher awareness, while we still can. Children mess up their room, but as they mature, they are more conscious of the need to keep it clean.

It is the very nature of a young soul planet, for those inhabiting it to desire a parent to guide and protect them. Dogmatic religious rules make them feel safe and protected. You are not expected to self-govern, when you are 3 or 4 years old. The basic rules are, "eat your veggies", "don't play in traffic", and "mind your parents". Praise or punishment is the expected reward for your actions. While we are on the Earth, that praise or punishment comes from outside our physical bodies. A young soul in the denseness of 3d reality, feels that reward or punishment comes from a parental god outside itself. Young children without strong parental figures, act out, hoping to find the safe boundaries of life in order to feel secure. Young souls seek a God outside themselves, to set their boundaries and dole out reward or punishment. Since rewards do not appear to be very just here on Earth, it is reasoned that they must be waiting for us in heaven. It is because of this sort of searching, that religions around the world have sprung up with similar stories. They comfort the children of God and make them feel safe, vindicated, blessed, or cursed. They are told that they are sheep, and need to give their power to a shepherd. The idea of self-responsibility is frightening. The expectations of responsibility begin around 4th grade. The Mayans tell us that we are in the 4th age, and moving into the 5th. In 5th grade, we will be responsible for turning in our own homework.

No one can deny that times are changing. Natural and manmade disaster appears to loom on the horizon. We need to embrace our power of choice. We must choose to be in these times of change, with acceptance and peace. We must choose to be better stewards of the Earth. We must choose to be as balanced as the animals that we share this planet with. While channeling, I was told that animal, vegetable, and mineral life come from 'hive' souls, which are very old souls that are in total touch with all others in the hive, both here and in other galaxies. We are likely children living amongst some very highly advanced beings of nature. If we listen to our elders, we might learn something. Nature holds us in her heart. She can be a gentle and loving parent, or a fierce taskmaster. Children should respect their elders. It really isn't nice to upset Mother Nature.

CHAPTER 5

StarSeeds

I f we can get away from the narrow idea that we are alone in the universe, then perhaps we will begin to start acting like responsible citizens of the universe. We might see a grander vision for ourselves than just this one planet. I am not trying to convince anyone that our fathers in heaven are aliens, because no matter where our seed came from, we are here now. What I am trying to get across is that we are all part of the cosmos in one way or another and expanding our mind to accept that possibility is helpful. I saw a Snoopy cartoon many years ago where Snoopy was looking up at the stars and saying how insignificant it made him feel. What if we could look up at the stars and know that we are part of a huge galactic family. Instead of insignificant, I would feel significant and powerful within my cosmic family.

Through channeling the energy called WE, I was given the understanding, that it is not uncommon for a superior race to bring a species forward and en-soul it. This process would take a procession around the galactic center, to allow for growth. The ones seeded appear to be, "Us". As the Bible says, "the sons of God saw the daughters of men, and they were pleased". Perhaps, those "daughters" of men got the seed and didn't know what happened to them. It would have seemed like a Virgin Birth.

If we are part alien, it would appear that we are trying to blend our instinctual animal nature with their more advanced or Spiritual nature. We could see ourselves as hybrids instead of lowbreds and that would be good for our self-esteem. Beings that are more advanced and able to traverse galaxies can seem better, or more Spiritual, than we are. They also know more of the total nature of the universe, than we do. We are earth-bound and therefore, have a limited vantage point. Their Spiritual or sacred energy may or may not be more advanced than ours. We do not know their hearts and intentions. I think that the alien races and the Earth race are all on a Spiritual path. It could be that they are further along in some aspects than we are, and perhaps, not as far in others.

Our society, as a whole, appears to still be very territorial and aggressive. Perhaps some alien races are also territorial and aggressive. I suspect that just as there is more than one race of human, there is more than one race of alien. It is logical that they each have their own agendas. They are certainly more technically advanced, as can be seen by the fact that they have star ships to get them around. I can certainly see how primitive people might easily have confused them with Gods.

I know I sound like the SCI FI channel, but we may be getting prepared by television, to accept what has been known for a very long time by a select few. Perhaps, it is within the power of our consciousness to awaken another strand or two of the "junk' DNA, which we have at our disposal. Some of the junk DNA that science has yet to unravel in our makeup, might be from our Skyfathers. I hope that it is time to take our step into the future, as citizens of Planet Earth, instead of ignorant and frightened animals. My main focus is on healing the addictions that plague this planet. Perhaps, seeing the larger picture of our oneness with all life in the galaxy will make hiding in addictive behaviors unnecessary.

I wonder how ignorant our animals really are. Some say that animals are lower life forms. I would like to say here, that I do not believe animals are lower than we are. In fact, it is likely the opposite; we are possibly the lowest life form on this planet. The ape is certainly in his right place in the natural scheme of things. We are the only ones fouling the water we need to drink, or polluting the air we need to breathe. (Cow flatulence not included)

Perhaps, the animal instinct that is being en-souled is an aggressive and territorial one. Or could it be true that our Sky Fathers were competitive and war-like? It certainly sounds like it, because there are many accounts of wars between the "gods" in biblical literature and mythology. I wonder who won in those wars, and what was the prize? Perhaps, the gentleness we are trying to find within ourselves comes, not from the Skygods, but from the mentality of the gentle Earth creatures. If that is true, then we are on Earth trying to fit our part alien consciousness, into a physical vehicle, with a monkey mind, in the denseness of matter and duality. Where is the *Easy*

Button when you need it? The missing link could easily be when the Skygods created us in their own image. This in no way takes away from the fact that we are all made of Godstuff. Everything and every Being, here or on other planets, has to be made from the Oneness of All that IS.

An alternative idea is that we are trying to blend our instinctive sexual nature with our Spiritual androgynous Godself. W.H. Church in his book * "Story of the Soul" uses the work of *Edgar Casey to explore the origins of our species going back to root races of Lemuria and Atlantis. Edgar Casey is a renowned psychic called "the sleeping prophet". He founded the Association of Research and Enlightenment, located on 66th and Atlantic in Virginia Beach, VA. Casey also speaks extensively about alien influence. If you would like to research this further, there are many great minds that have written of times in the distant past, when it appears that this planet was visited by an alien race.

"Zachariah Stitchen", in * "The 12th Planet, and his many other works on the subject, offers a wealth of information about our Alien origins. His Sumerian translations made it clear that a race of Aliens, coming from a planet called Nibiru, visited and seeded this planet to create miners. They needed gold for their atmosphere and did not want to do the physical labor. His work was first discredited as a fool's folly, until our own space program confirmed some of his translations. When our own space crafts returned to Earth, they proved that what he had translated from Cuneiform text was indeed accurate. There would have been no way of acquiring the information that had been written eons ago, unless it was viewed from outer space, while landing on our planet. Just as the cuneiform text reported, there is geological evidence that a nuclear explosion leveled the Middle East thousands of years ago. There is ample evidence, and scientific findings, that will give you plenty of information on these geological events. The history channel runs a television series called Ancient Aliens, which explores this theory in great detail. They too, are talking about Wars between the Gods. Perhaps the prize was and may still be, Earth.

There have been ET (extra-terrestrial) sightings as far back as the beginning of recorded history. There are figures of spacemen drawn in Neanderthal caves. The television is full of conspiracy theories, about how we have covered up spacecraft crashes, and reverse engineered the technology. I have no doubt, that there have been such crashes. The evidence is plentiful and compelling.

Because of all the misinformation and conspiracy theories, it seems likely to me that aliens have visited this planet and that it is known at higher levels than the public is privy to. I doubt that we have very much to fear. It would make sense that if the alien races wanted us dead, we would have been dead by now. Unlike in the movies, our defenses are likely child's play to the vastness and strength of our universal family. One thing that sticks out glaringly to me is that if they are here, they are not overly concerned about the state of our existence, nor of our planet's pollution. If they are concerned, they may not be able to fix it, or they are just waiting for us to leave, so they can clean up our mess.

I was talking to someone about all this, and he was adamant that he was an **Earth Man.** He didn't want anything to do with the Skygods. He had been talking about the possibility that the Greek Gods were actually aliens. I told him I was fairly sure, that if we were not part Skygod, we would still be sitting under a tree, picking fleas off our mates. (He was not happy with that logic). It is undeniable that our evolutionary curve took a giant leap to get us where we are so quickly. They have now proven Darwin's theory to be wrong. Apparently, we showed up here much like we currently are and did not evolve from apes

I feel that we have been kept in the dark regarding the knowledge of our sky brothers. Maybe the powers above us fear that we would use our fight or flight response and chaos would ensue. Or perhaps, they don't want to admit that we were just one of many races, not all that wonderful and powerful. I have seen reports that we have attempted to shoot at a UFO. That certainly wasn't very neighborly, but it was probably more like a child shooting a toy pistol at a train. Another scenario might be: if we had the knowledge of who we really are- we would not need the goods and services of those on this planet who feed off us.

It really is of no consequence, regarding where we came from, or from which species we get our strength, and which gives us our gentleness. What really matters is how we can blend these two basic instincts, and come forth into a new age of awareness and peace. We must cure the scourge of addiction and violence that plagues this planet if we are to go forward at all. The fight or flight response is certainly useful, but not to be blindly followed in the New Age. We are no longer the hunter or the hunted. We are (hopefully) shedding the cloud of unknowing, preparing to participate on a planetary level, with other beings, in other galaxies. This appears to me to be our goal.

There are many predictions about what will happen in the coming new age. There are facets of society that are attempting to prepare for Earth Changes and disasters of all kinds. We have survivalists hiding out with guns and rations. We have people with tin foil hats waiting for the UFO's to suck out their brains and others that want to be beamed up to the mother-ship. We have people trying to gather vast amounts of money, thinking that they can control others with pieces of paper. Everybody is aware of world disasters, and getting frightened by dire predictions. If the poles are shifting, and the world is ending, there isn't much we can do about it -so why not create happiness until then. If there is the slightest chance that being on the positive side of duality by being happy and spreading joy will change the outcome of our transition into the coming age, why not give it a try? Certainly, being peacefully in the awareness of our Soul will take much of the fear out of our journey.

By the way; **the poles have shifted before, and the Earth is still here**. If you don't believe this, just ask any geologist that has studied past Earth cycles.

Maybe, one day the mother ship will land on the white house lawn, and we will all know what is really going on. Maybe they will tell us who we are, and where we came from. In truth it doesn't matter, because we all come from the same place. We are from within God, and we are made of God-stuff.... I still want to know what our place in the Universe is. I hope we are old enough as a species, to find out. I hope we have grown enough to stop shooting first. Perhaps, we are being protected by our own government, or by a race of aliens residing on this planet, from an evil alien invasion. I would still want to know it! I hope that this is the time of our awakening to our place in the Universal family and that we will really be able to become Citizens of the Universe.

Rev. Lorana Clark

My Alien Experiences

I have had personal experiences with what appeared to me to be alien encounters but, they are not nearly as elaborate or detailed as some I have read. Events such as these don't really frighten me; they merely seem "interesting". I have awakened on two different occasions to the presence of "alien" beings by my bed. Once, I woke up to find three smallish grey hooded figures at the foot of my bed. Another time, I woke to find a blue Being beside my bed that appeared to be nothing but vibrant energy. On the first encounter I said nothing, but the next time I summoned all my energy to be able to say, "What". When I did that, everything just disappeared. Thinking back I wonder if that was Archangel Michael, because his energy is that same electric blue. I broke the connection when I "*just had to speak.*" I felt the overwhelming urge to have the power to be *able* to speak. I was shaken by both of these events, and did not return to sleep. I am certain I was not "just dreaming".

In one instance, I remembered being on some kind of metal table, looking to the side and seeing a baby carrier, with little booty feet showing over the edge. The curious thing was that they were three toed bird type feet, with perfect little booties made to fit. I am not sure if I was dreaming or if this really happened, because I believe I have been "taken" on numerous occasions. I could have also been remembering another lifetime.

On one occasion, I found myself coming back to the Earth on some kind of a craft. I was looking out the window, and commenting on what didn't look right about the North American continent. I was shown a map that said I was looking at the Sea of California. This body of water came in behind the Baja peninsula, and spread all the way up to the salt lake. I have no idea if I was experience a distant past, or a future.

While having an out of body experience, I was on an enclosed steel deck with observation windows. I came upon a being, looking out the window. I knew that I was just exploring, and wanted a closer look. I thought I could go unnoticed. This being was very strange. He looked like a big upright crocodile with a birdlike head. Later I learned it could have been the Crocodile God Sobek. It could have, just as easily, been Horus or Thoth, because of the feathered head and the birdlike mouth. It could also have been, none of the above, but the overall energy was reptilian. He had the strangest eyes I have ever seen. They were iridescent turquois, with light green where our white is. They were slit, and had tear ducts, like in a drawing of the eye of Horus, which were wet against shiny black and green feathers. Its mouth looked like a cross between a parrot's and a croc's. It turned out, that I was not invisible to him, and he was <u>not</u> happy to see me. He made a shrieking noise at me, and it scared me right back into my body. I got the feeling that I was trespassing, OOPS! Very sorry to be snooping around your observation deck, your Godship ....*I'll be going now*!

CHAPTER 6

Paying Attention

Now that we have explored the possibility that we are StarSeeds, let's begin to look at what we can do with these ideas. If indeed we are beings that came from another star system or the result of breeding with a species between the Earth and the Star people, it follows that we are more than we may have thought ourselves to be. Can we use this information to improve our condition? It appears that awareness of who we are will help us do just that. One of the most compelling ideas being put forward now is that we are able to create events with just our thoughts, by using natural laws. One does not have to look very far to find a book or a class on positive thinking or creative visualization. With just a little exploration it becomes evident that we are indeed creative beings. This is because we are conceived within the creative force of the entire Universe. It is our lineage to be creative. Actually, we create events all the time, it is impossible not to create our experiences. The task is to do it consciously, instead of by default.

If we realize that we are creative Spiritual beings, and not just the body we reside in, we can step out of our little self, gain a new perspective and begin to work consciously, within the illusion of duality. We can create balance and harmony for ourselves and our planet. We will then be worthy of taking our place as, "Citizens of the Universe". Perhaps, the end of the Mayan calendar signals a time when the veil between our world and others is lifted, and we become aware of our true nature. Can we control the fight or flight response of our instinctual nature? Can we progress into a new era of human development, in the face of natural disasters and perhaps, alien contact and influence?

Many of us believe that we are alone in the universe, and still believe in superstitious dogma. These beliefs will have to be examined if we are to change our current paradigm. We also believe that we can obtain power through a currency called money. Any first year student of economics will tell you that our monetary systems are based on illusion. Our belief is what we _pay_ attention with, and our currency is really <u>our valuable attention</u>. No amount of paper money is as powerful as our full attention. *What we pay attention to grows and what we ignore diminishes. Therein lies the secret to all manifestation and healing.*

We should not ignore the everyday world, but it is no longer just about our job, or our looks, or our status. It is important to get our heads in the right place, and create a healing, helping environment where everyone has equal citizenship in our universal family. I am not suggesting that you join a community action group to save the whales, or walk for the cure. Actively participating in a positive movement can be uplifting, as long as it is pro instead of against what your passion is. You need to understand that focusing your valuable attention, on what you think should be happening, is wonderful and worthy. Placing your valuable attention on, "fighting" what you don't want only *pays* for more of it and you get more of it.

Anyone who has ever been involved in a traditional 12 step program knows that they must "turn it over" and trust their Higher Power if they want to overcome their addictive behavior. When you turn something over to a Higher Power you are getting in touch with the God force within and expecting good results. If you use your own will power to fight against your addiction constantly thinking about what you don't want to do, you end up doing that very thing. Any behavior or circumstance can be changed by focusing on what you choose instead of what you don't choose. When many minds are thinking of the same thing results must follow. If you are focusing on the *"aint it awfuls"* they will surely become stronger. I invite you to THINK about what you are always thinking about, because that is what you are creating for yourself, your family and the world.

There are many books about helping you find wealth, health and happiness through positive thinking. This is not one of them; those are good and valuable tools, but only part of the picture. Our goal is corralling our monkey mind, harness the power of our SoulSelf, and learn to bring that forth. Effects such as health, wealth, and healthy relationships are bonuses in the process. I would like to invite you to really think about what it would be like, not to be under the pressure of the *have-to's,* and the *can't-do's.* Imagine learning that we are all part of a Universal family and our family supports our every need. What if, we learn that our goals can change from feeding our body, to feeding our souls? Soul food would be easy to focus on if you didn't have to be in survival mode all the time. By changing the focus of our collective thinking we can have our physical needs met and focus on our spiritual growth. There is enough of everything to go around if the world would share. On this Young Soul Planet we must learn to share our toys.

CHAPTER 7

The Law of Attraction

The Law of Attraction states that what we think about we bring about, when fused with intent and emotion. What we continually think about becomes a core belief, and becomes entrenched in our subconscious mind. It is from the subconscious mind that we attract our personal reality, so the trick is to plant new thought seeds in the subconscious. New beliefs in the subconscious attract better results in our life circumstances. In order to help ourselves graduate from this Earth School we must learn that we are attracting our life circumstances, and then learn how to do so consciously. We must learn to pay attention and attract what we want, instead of what we don't want. The Law of Attraction is not a new concept. It has been understood by many great thinkers through the ages. It has gained popularity in recent years due to the plethora of new age gurus who have been able to get their message across to the public. Let us all give a round of applause to the internet for that! The internet has created a one world information system. The New Thought message is flooding the airways.. The law of attraction is also gaining popularity, because of movies like* "The Secret".

Emotion, intent and gratitude are the tools of attraction. Emotions supercharge prayer of any kind. I believe that emotions are the tantalizing, almost addictive, stuff that makes taking on a physical life so tempting and alluring. Pick up any book on manifestation or the law of attraction, and you will soon learn that emotion is a key player in creating what you choose to have, be, or do. I feel that many people who study the law of attraction get stuck in the acquisition of things. It is true that we can attract what we want, but ultimately it is more important to learn who is doing the attracting and how the process works.

Here on this planet we teach ourselves with the illusion of duality. We experience what we don't want so that we can come to an understanding of what we do want. We can do that in reverse if we choose, but seldom do we experience what we want first. You can go from the have-nots to the haves, the lonely to the loved-- all through events seemingly outside of yourself. Once you understand that you have attracted the circumstances of your life, you can choose to attract differently. I say, it is true that you can be, do, or have anything you choose with emotion, intent, and gratitude. I add that it will be within the scope of your personal life contract. That would be the one you made prior to this lifetime. (More about this later)

If your soul's purpose is better served by living in a modest but comfortable home, rather than the mansion on the hill, you will not override your higher life intention. It would be a waste of your time to create the mansion, and shirk your intentions for a particular lifetime. Your guides and Higher Self will nudge you toward your destination, without denying you free will. On a young soul planet the guides are on active duty, and very busy. I believe that no matter what experiences we choose on a soul level, each of us is entitled to comfort in this life. We will begin to have it, the moment that we can start learning in any other way than through discomfort or dis-ease. The Evangelical minister is right when he says that we always have the 'favor' of the Lord, and we are his blessed children. If you have the 'favor' of the Lord, it won't help you much if you don't know enough to accept it. Having a "New Thought" of acceptance and thanksgiving is what allows us to accept the gifts that are already ours. Yes you read that right, all the gifts are already ours, given by the creator of the entire universe. It is up to us to choose what ones we would like to experience. A gift is "experience" and we get to choose what kind of experience of life we would like through the law of attraction.

It is pretty hard to seek Spiritual enlightenment, while the alligators are snapping at your heels. You think you must take care of the pressing issues of the physical body, such as food and shelter before you have time for Spirituality. *It is **the quest for Spiritual knowledge, and the understanding of the law of attraction that gets the alligators off your heels.*** After you have tried all the same old ways of dealing with your circumstances, think about trying something different. It is when things go bad that many of us cry 'bad luck" or blame

God, or say that we are suffering now, so we can have a high place in heaven. We need to rationalize the craziness of our experiences in some way, so we either blame God or claim God because of them.

Some people believe that if they are good folk, and give to the church and to others, they will be OK. The laws of attraction are such that if your belief in anything is strong enough, it will be the truth for you. Tithing works, if you believe in it. Salvation works, if you believe in it. Biting the head off a chicken works, if you believe it will. I am not trying to take away from any form of Religion or philosophy. Once we become aware of the law of attraction we know that it is the *belief in them* that makes them work. Being a good and responsible person will work well for you, if your underlying belief is in the goodness of life. If you are being good because you are afraid not to be, your self -esteem needs help, and your fears will manifest. Negative beliefs, and karma, are the reasons bad things happen to good people. We can change our negative beliefs and create better circumstances in our lives. Our karma is interwoven into our life journey before we incarnate. We can change how we experience seemingly negative karmic events and thereby experience them as less negative or tragic.

As I said before, fear is an emotion and is one of the names of duality therefor; by the law of attraction, if you fear something strongly enough, you will bring what you fear to your door. If you are an accomplished thief, and truly believe that you are Robin Hood-- it is your belief that will keep you out of jail. In my philosophy called New Thought, we often call our kindness to others *paying forward*. We know that we will receive as we give, but perhaps not from the same source. When circumstances in life get challenging, instead of bemoaning our luck, we always look for the messages they are mirroring back to us. If we attracted a negative circumstance it must have come from within, and we can follow it to its source and change our inner beliefs.

I must preface these next two paragraphs, with the assurance that I do not believe everyone that is ill, or has been victimized is consciously at fault. I wish to illustrate how subconscious programs can make you sick, drunk, battered or broke, because of some deep seated pattern that is at work in our pain body. Our pain body is the baggage that we carry around in our subconscious. I will go further into depth about pain bodies later.

We become victims because of our core beliefs. Many people cherish their suffering. They hold on to it for dear life. It is their suffering that makes them feel special. I say, "Ok go for it, if it serves you". I am not here to steal your pain. I will help you leave it behind if you choose to. For some people, there can be a big payoff to being a victim. It's not your "fault" that way. *He did it,* or *she made me do it,* are all excuses for not taking personal responsibility. You can then be just an innocent victim of circumstances. Victimhood is also liberating; you "can't because" you have health issues, or you have no money, you're not that smart or your partner won't "let you". You are the victim, and someone else has to do the unwelcome task for you. I'm so sorry for you, NOT. I have the utmost *compassion* for you, and I will help you see a different truth for yourself if you choose to do so. The blame game has big payoffs in addictive behaviors. Addiction use victim consciousness to keep you stuck in its clutches, always wanting you to blame outer circumstances for your habits.

You will continually attract into your life the kind of people and circumstances that you resonate to. You will attract relationships into your life that show you what you expect for yourself. Personal relationships will mirror all your hidden stuff. On the other hand, IF you can change the deep subprograms in your mind, you can begin to attract different results in your outer life. Your personal relationships will become much healthier and rewarding. The sum and total of your beliefs about life are sent forth from your energy field, and attract the answer to your inner belief. You must change your comfort zone if you are not happy with the one you are in. It is your expectations, and your deep seated beliefs, that place you on the path of what you choose in life. Everything is choice, whether you choose consciously or by default. What you have brought into this life experience from Spirit, and what you have accumulated as fact since you arrived, is all before you in the form of your current situation. Hence the statement we often use, "you are in your right place by right of your own consciousness". If you don't like the place you are in, change your consciousness.

If you want to know the climate of any person's consciousness, just look at their life and you will see what they believe about themselves. If your life is a mess, clean your closets, and get rid of the outer clutter. In that way the inner clutter will be cleansed also. If you don't like something that you have attracted, you can bet that it is something you need to look at within yourself. When we look at our relationships, who we attract as mates often tells us what our strongest lessons are. Relationships are the best way to have your inner climate challenged by outer circumstances. Once I understood this, I realized that those who came into my life were a reflection of my inner journey. I was then able to use that knowledge to change my life. I learned some heavy lessons about my inner climate through my personal relationships, for which I am now totally thankful. Once I saw my pattern, I could choose whether I wanted it or not. Just knowing what is drawing situations to you, can be all the healing you need. If the light of awareness does not change your circumstances by itself, you have to begin actively giving yourself a new belief. In any addictive pattern, learning what deep belief drives the addictive behavior will go a long way to help keep the behavior in check. True healing of addictions does not happen until the cause of the problem is also healed.

Of course, not all patterns are negative. You might be a child protégé, and be drawing things and events to you that remind you of your talents. On the contrary, if you are working on healing the victim in you, victim is what you will see, until you purge it from your program. If comfortable and happy is what you have deep within you, events and people will come into your life that will enhance comfortable and happy. You will bring them to you by the law of attraction. Obviously comfort and happiness is the desirable state of being, but you have to create that place within yourself, before it can manifest in your outer world. This is why everyone always says that you have to love yourself, before someone else can love you.

We are also told that the only person we can change is ourselves. You are in charge of your _conscious mind._ You can change the field of energy that is around you by planting new thought seeds in your conscious mind. Each time the energy swirls around you it begins to pick up the new crop of thoughts, instead of the old habits that are being replaced.

Pretty soon the climate of your energy is attracting different people, places, and things into your life. Affirmations and post-its on the mirror can help you plant new seeds in your conscious mind. Affirmations are reminders to have a new thought about who you are and what you choose.

Our conscious mind is the gateway to the subconscious. Beliefs that we pick up have to be viewed consciously before they can get planted in the subconscious. When we are toddlers we take what others say about us or what our circumstances are as the truth of our life. Our conscious mind does not have a critical factor strongly in place when we are very young. Therefore, we take what authority figures label us as gospel. The childhood circumstances shape our adult life until we examine them and purge what does not serve us any longer. Where trouble starts is when they go unchecked and produce negative beliefs. Those beliefs will keep validating themselves by being attracted over and over again just like a magnet.

The mechanics of your magnetic personality

The diagram below shows the circles of energy swirling around you. As the energy whirls it picks up programming from the remembered past, and the subconscious past, as well as from past lives, and the intent of the OverSoul. These energies create a climate that attracts other similar energy climates to it. We are not moving into the future, we are attracting it to us. The way it works is similar to magnetism...

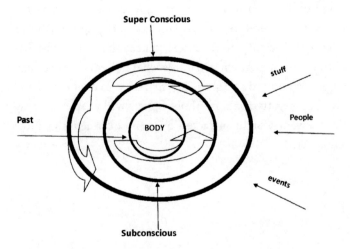

Affirmation;

I watch in detached wonderment, the events that unfold in my life, knowing that on some level, I have attracted them.

Your energy field swirls around you all the time. It is often referred to as the auric field. You are a ball of energy, attracting like energy to you at all times. What determines what you attract is what is already present in this field of energy. With each revolution of energy, we pick up a reminder from Spirit, or the super conscious, about what our game plan is. We then blend that with the experiential memories that we can recall. They then get processed against what is held in the subconscious mind. It is in the subconscious mind that past life memories are available, and it is also where the pain body lives. Any trauma carried over from another lifetime, or talent carried forth works its way to the surface, and is demonstrated in life events.

CHAPTER 8

Auras and Chakras

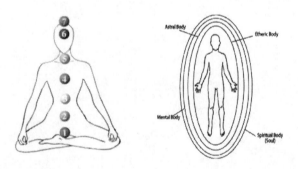

T he ball of energy that surrounds you and helps attract like energy to you is called your Aura or Auric field. Our aura is the swirling energy body that we live in. It appears to encase us in an egg-like membrane. . I have seen auras around people that were all prickly, all slushy, or all bright and shiny. The perception most of us have is that we have an aura; however it is more descriptive to say that our aura has us. We are the nucleus of this energy egg that we reside in. It is through the aura that we resonate with others and attract like energy to like energy. The colors of the aura represent the different chakras of our body. Chakra is the name for a swirling vortex of energy that is generated by your body. There are 7 basic Chakras which are loosely associated with the endocrine system. They start at the base of your spine, and go up to the crown of your head. Each Chakra is connected to a physical center, and is associated with a color of the rainbow. These energy centers are moving and flowing around you all the time. One of the ways that we can help heal ourselves is by cleansing our aura. Some people can see the colors of the aura around people and things. It does not matter if you can see your aura or not, it is enough to know that it exists. We now know that thoughts are purposeful therefor; it is possible to do mental exercises to polish up your aura and get rid of negative junk that might be hanging around in it. Doing meditation to cleanse the aura will help mend your outer circumstances.

You can view your aura by using Kirlian photography, which many metaphysical centers have available for their clientele. If your aura is cloudy or one color is out of balance, it tells you where you need balance in the corresponding area of your physical body and also in your life experiences. Our aura reflects our emotional, mental, and physical health. It is much easier to effect and heal the aura, once you realize that you are already inside it. You don't have to reach out and get it. You have to sit down and be in it consciously. By cleansing your aura with colored light and soft music coupled with creative imagination and visualization, you can bring health, happiness, peace, and joy into your life.

The following is a brief description of your aura colors and what they affect.

Root Chakra; Red

The colors associated with the aura and energy body begin at the base of your spine with red, which is the energy that grounds you to the Earth. This chakra is associated with the fight or flight response of our survival instinct when danger is imminent. When your red energy is out of balance you are feeling threatened and you feel the need for protection. A good healthy base or root chakra is essential to live peacefully among others on the planet. It maintains your boundaries and creates aggressive energy when threatened. Many people have the idea that aggression is wrong. Passivity is not the road to Spirituality, acceptance is. There will be times when you need to respond with your aggressive energy, or know when to get out of the way of the bus.

Eastern philosophy labels the life-force energy located in the first chakra as the Kundalini. Strong Spiritual experiences or states of deep meditation move this energy up your core, and brings with it a state of total bliss. Orgasmic sexual satisfaction can move the Kundalini up the spine and bring about a strong sexual/Spiritual experience. This Kundalini energy is also known as the Serpent or the Phoenix. The serpent got a bad name from the early Christians, who felt guilty about sex and equated the serpent with their devil and sexuality. The Phoenix rises from the ashes to the height of human expression.

Creative Chakra; Orange

The second chakra is your orange energy. This is your reproductive and creative center. Satisfaction or frustration resides here. This energy is in the middle of your lower body, between your survival instinct and your emotional instinct. It is from here you create everything. It is the seat of sexual energy, and so much more. Orange is the color of physical manifestation. The Reiki healing modality uses the color orange to begin all healing work, because it is from your second chakra that you keep your physical body's energy intact. It is from here that you create a child in both the male and the female body, therefor orange is fundamental to life-force energy.

The second chakra is also the energy we use to create art and music. It is the seat of imagination, which is one of the voices of God within us. While in the total absorption of creative work this chakra glows. You feel in the "zone" when you are doing what you love with the deepest of intent. When the creative juices are flowing, happiness and contentment are the bi-products.

Emotional Chakra; Yellow

This chakra is the seat of emotions and it is yellow. This is the feeling chakra from which we mourn our losses and feel our fears. It is from this Chakra that compassion, and passion for self and others is felt. This is the top rung of the instinctual or animal energy. These three lower chakras are what we crave in the physical. It is very hard to get in touch with our SoulSelf if these chakras are not working properly. You have to be grounded to live successfully on Earth. A seed must be in nourishing soil before it can rise up to meet the sun. The instinctual chakras are the bedrock of your physical existence. When addiction is present, these three energy centers are most certainly out of balance.

Many of us are afraid of our emotions. You might never choose to risk loving someone again, because the end of a relationship was so hurtful. We often try to escape our negative emotions. We can dull our emotional response in many different legal and illegal ways, but the underlying emotion is still there and will fester until dealt with. If you learned your lessons about relationships you need not worry about being so devastated by them again. It is only when you can "*feel through*" the painful experiences that you become balanced in this chakra.

All emotions are not negative, but the negative ones seem to be the ones we pay most of our valuable attention to. When the third chakra is overworked it sends a signal to the first chakra that danger of loss is imminent. That is the recipe for reacting to life instead of acting in life.

The instinctual energy is animal energy and the survival of the fittest prevails. These Chakras are connected to the reptile brain at the base of our neck. (*There is a bit of lizard in all of us*). Kundalini as the serpent creates sexual fulfillment, while Kundalini as the Phoenix rises toward the crown and brings Spiritual fulfillment. The instinctual chakras automatically respond to each other and work from the bottom up. If we feel physically threatened we often panic and our reasoning processes either freeze or go into high gear. We go into survival mode and respond with our animal instincts. When we are sexually or creatively stifled the neighboring chakras feel the heat and react adversely. Finding something to stimulate your creative energy every day will help your entire life experience. You could play music, dance, sculpt, or write, anything to be creative, and use those chakras constructively. Above all do not be afraid to be yourself. Ah yes,.. but first it is good to find out who that is.

Heart Chakra; Green

The next chakra is the seat of the soul which is Green energy. It is the heart chakra and from here we connect with the energy of love. The fourth chakra is the mixing bowl that blends the bottom three physical chakras with the top three. It is in the heart that we actually blend the instinctual being with the Spiritual being. The marriage between our higher SoulSelf and our animal nature happens in the heart. It is the most important chakra, because without the heart nothing else matters.

I believe that this chakra is connected to every other heart energy alive, on or off of this planet. It is the heart-mind. Inspiration comes through this chakra. It is one of the three voices of God in action and I believe it is the most important one. When we learn to live from our heart and not our fear, life takes on an entirely new meaning. Simple pleasures are delightful. A smile is our normal countenance and joy is our contribution to life.

Fear cannot live in the heart energy when it is clear and healthy. If you keep your heart closed for very long it attacks you and you could physically die. When you begin to move into your heart energy you will eliminate the paralyzing fear of the material world that you used to think mattered so much.

When living from the heart chakra, the bottom three chakras and the top three chakras can be balanced and work in unison. Life is sacred and life is sweet. It is from the heart chakra that unconditional love is possible. Physical love is limiting and demands satisfaction and payment for its emotional expenditure. Unconditional love is non-particular and loves all aspects of duality equally.

An affirmation came to me while I was practicing being in my heart chakra. I say practicing because few of us are avatars or advanced Yogis. The knowledge that we can even do such a thing as live in the heart energy is a great gift in itself. The more we practice and the more we stay in this energy, the less we feel the effects of the fears and worries of the world.

Affirmation

I am the energy of all life, I am connected to
"All that IS", I am Spirit, and I reside in my heart.

Throat Chakra; Blue

Above the heart is the fifth chakra, which is blue. It is from here that we have the gift of speech. Our ability to name and claim things comes from this chakra. Our personal power and ego are expressed from here. It is the first chakra above the heart which separates us from our instinctual nature. When we are emotionally stable, and have a healthy self-esteem, we are able to speak our truth quietly and clearly. There is no need for fan-fare, or screaming and shouting. We are not afraid to let the world know who we are.

When this center is out of balance we do not speak our truth. We defend our position with anger and fear. If you are not a screamer, you may be shy and self-effacing. You prefer to stay in the shadows, hoping no one will notice you and see your deficiencies. Social posturing and the need for the approval of others is overpowering when you blend the fifth chakra with the third, in an unhealthy way. This is what is labeled "the pack mentality". It is as if the heart is bypassed and the fit between the Instinctual being and the Spiritual being is out of sync. The only way you can speak your truth is if you have the backup of your pack.

It is said that the "Gods" gave us the gift of speech. Perhaps this is one of the genetic alterations that was made by the Skygods. We strive to become Citizens of the Universe and a healthy blending of our animal nature with our SoulSelf is vital to our survival and our graduation as a species, into Citizens of the Universe.

Third-eye Chakra; Indigo

The sixth chakra is the third eye, it is indigo. It is from here that the gift of intuition resides. When the third eye is open we can see through the veil, as the old Spiritualists call it. The veil is the separation between the physical and the nonphysical world. When babies are born there is a membrane over their face which is said to be a veil. The old wives tale says that if the veil is torn the child will have psychic abilities. The reason for this is that the third eye, or the sixth chakra, would be exposed and the window to see into the other world is open.

I am reminded of the energetic membrane that is around the Aura. We can open our third eye, and peek at the other side, but if we can't close the curtain again and go about our daily life, a problem arises. Many of the metaphysical enthusiasts' desperately want to open the third eye, but don't have the rest of their life balanced. It is possible, but not advisable, to do so without first balancing the entirety of your energy field.

This is the chakra most affected by the use of drugs and alcohol. Ripping this chakra open artificially can invite dark energy from the astral plane into your auric field and cause havoc in your life. Not all energy is positive in the astral plane just as all energy is not positive on the physical one. It is in the third eye that our conscious mind is linked with our intuitive mind or sixth sense. When this chakra is open, we have a clear intuition, and can get information from the Spiritual realm. Our guides have easier access to our conscious mind when this chakra is clear. If this center is not functioning normally, whether it is open or not, we can become mentally unbalanced.

The third eye does not have to be open for a person to have a balanced life. A young soul can bump along and believe that chance, or luck, or Jesus is guiding their steps. They can be content in whatever belief system is available in their society. On a young soul planet there are many sheep. Sheep are gentle animals that need their shepherd to protect them from the wolves. It is not necessary to grow into an avatar in one lifetime. What is necessary is to have a balanced chakra system so you can grow in love and happiness. Young souls are not expected to mature in one lifetime. What is important is that they are well-adjusted children.

The second chakra aligns with this center, and together they blend the two voices of God, Imagination and Intuition with the heart chakra which is Inspiration. If both are put in equal measure into the heart, a beautiful symphony of Spirit is experienced. The inspired life is then available to the SoulSelf.

Crown Chakra; White, pink, or purple

The top physical chakra is the crown, which is seen as pink, white, or a light purple. I believe it depends on the nature of the soul. It is from this chakra that we can conceptualize God. This chakra is the counterpart of the first chakra. It is our direct connection to the Spiritual realms just as the first chakra is our direct connection to the Earth Goddess.

When this chakra is open and working well we feel connected to "All that IS". Our Spirit guides and Higher Self have easy access to our life path. Synchronicity is the normal state of being. We feel at one with our source. The Kundalini energy rises out of this chakra and touches the Spirit world. Miracles are sent from our guides into this center. St. Theresa went into ecstasy with an open crown chakra.

Trance-Channeled energy comes in through this chakra. Fortunately this chakra, being the connection to the Higher Self, has protection. You could say that the "Guardians" reside here. Thankfully, our Higher Self knows better than to let unwanted energy into our body at this level.

When all our chakras are clear and clean our energy ball is a beautiful rainbow. The energy around us is not stagnant. It changes color with our moods. Our aura is a giant mood ring that is ever changing. When we are sad, mad, or sick the energy can get brown and muddy in spots. A person that can see the aura can tell you where you need balance in your life.

To find out what color your aura is you can use your powerful imagination. Close your eyes and notice the first color you witness. At first black or red usually is all you'll see. If that happens, wait a minute and you will get a hint of another color in your mind and imagination.

On a subconscious level we are interacting with each another's auras all the time. I offer a workshop on aura painting. Each person in the class takes turns being the subject. The others in the class use water colors to paint what colors they perceive around the subject. The similarities are amazing when everyone compares their work.

CHAPTER 9

OverSouls

We are Souls that have Bodies, not Bodies that have Souls

I f energy never dies, but is always changing like scientists tell us, and life is energy, then life must be eternal. *Life is eternal, but obviously bodies are not.* It is also obvious that we are not our body, but what enlivens it. We are the immortal soul within it. I believe that the entirety of humanity belongs to an OverSoul. I use the term OverSoul to portray this larger entity that we are part of. We are fragments of an OverSoul. When I was first learning to channel, I kept getting an old song in my head. It was, "♫ Get a Message from Michael ♫". Shortly after that, I ran into a book series called, "Messages from Michael" by Chelsea Quinn Yarbro. The Michael teachings call souls, "fragments", and categorize them into soul types. It is a fascinating series of work. These distinctions are really not important, but convenient to wrap our head around the concept of whom we are on a soul level, and what our goals might be.

One of the things I often hear from people is, "I need to find my soul's purpose". I believe the main purpose of incarnating is to learn and grow. I believe our purpose is to learn to choose consciously. Do you choose to add to the pool of joy, or add to the pool of fear, while you are here in the land of duality? Undoubtedly, we will add to one or the other pools by default, whether we are aware of it or not. Our life experience is a gift to the OverSoul that we are a part of. Imagine the gift that a happy life is, to the totality of our OverSoul. Now ask yourself, what kind of harm a life of misery can do. The idea that suffering is somehow noble is off the mark. It literally is your duty to be happy, so that happiness grows for the rest of us.

One of the first and most important truths I have learned is that we are here to share with others about who we are and the things we learn. Our personal progress is really part of the collective progress. Helping others seems to be a very fulfilling experience. By helping others we are actually, helping ourselves, as part of the OverSoul. We are to understand that the "we" not the "I" is the important part of life. At the same time, I can say that if the "I" is not made special and cherished the "we" will suffer. Let's remember that we are all in this together, from the most ignorant to the most intelligent. We are all part of the God-stuff that created us and beats our heart at this very moment. Our purpose here is individual and collective.

If I were to compare my entire physical body to a single cell within it, I would instantly become aware of the importance of the health and wellbeing of that single cell. It only takes one cell to create a disease like cancer. It has been proven, many times, that the ideas and the emotional environment of the human being affect its entire organism. The jingle, ♫ "Don't worry, be happy" ♫, is wise and healthy advice. Perhaps the Rastafarians are on to something!

The health and wellbeing of one soul, affects the health and wellbeing of the entire OverSoul. It may be helpful to imagine that, to each cell, your body is the OverSoul, *sort of a mini you*. To your body, the full expression of self, in Spirit, is the OverSoul, *your Higher Self*. To that Higher Self, the entire human race is the OverSoul and to it, all of creation is the OverSoul... To creation, there is God, the one and only source of *"All that IS"*.

We are taught by our ministers that we are trying to get into heaven and be with God. It has been said, in many different ways that no one will be left behind. It is literally all or nothing. That does not give you license to whip your neighbors into shape, so you can go. What you could do instead, is set a good example by being happy. Happiness or sorrow spreads to others. This is the expanded hundred monkey theory.

How could someone be left behind, if we are all part of the one first cause and we are made from God-stuff? We can't get out of God, no matter how hard we try. You can't be separate from ""All that IS"". If it is true that we can't spiritually advance without every soul advancing, we need to create a "critical mass" of others desiring the same goal. I use the following example to help people grasp this concept. This analogy uses one human body to represent the entire human race.

The TOUL Story.

Imagine trying to climb the stairs and leaving your big toe on the bottom step. It would not work to cut off your toe, because in this analogy, you can kill the body, but not the *toul*.(Here is where the critical mass thinking comes in). If the larger part of your total being is at the top of the stairs, your toe has no choice but to follow. Once at the top of the stairs your toe becomes aware of how great it is at the top of the stairs. It no longer desires to stay at the bottom, where it thought it was safe and secure, and had all those pretty shoes to wear. The toe finds out that it is free to be *toul*. *(Toe tapping soul music) Toe + Soul = Toul*

When the majority of the human race is aware of its true nature as souls with bodies, instead of bodies with souls, the rest of the race will 'get it' also. Many New Age and New Thought philosophers tell us that what is at the top of the stairs is our 'light-body', and we are going to transform into it. It makes me think of a Spirit that has a form, but not substance. A Spirit can walk through walls, and appears to telepathically send information. If we believe in the stories of alien encounters it appears that aliens can do the same thing. We could also speculate that perhaps, it is not our individual soul fragments that will be ascending to a light body, but the entire OverSoul that we are a part of. That is a very big idea and if it is true, all we can do is our part to make the totality of our OverSoul succeed. The best you can do is to bring joy into your life expression, no matter what the larger agenda might be. Tough Job: somebody has to do it, so it might as well be you.

CHAPTER 10

We are Godlings

God, "All that IS" and Oneness are words that attempt to describe the creator of everything, and to convey the idea that we cannot get outside of "All that IS". These words help us conceptualize something that is really beyond the understanding of our little monkey minds. Without the clear understanding of the oneness of all life, no matter what you call it, there is little hope that we can move into the new Age with any kind of Grace. Hopefully, enough people will understand what Jesus meant when he said, "what you do to the least of you; you do to me also". If we are all fragments of one creative soul, and come from one energy, which is life, love, God, (*pick a name*) and if we don't play nice with each other, we will all lose. What is one of the first things we learn as children? "Share your toys"! If this were not a *young soul planet* we would know how to share our food, and how to fulfill the necessary needs of each individual. On this planet we are learning to, "do unto others as you would have them do unto you," and to share the resources with all. I am not promoting some sort of political agenda. I am talking about the deepest level of understanding that, if I hurt you, or deprive you, or shame you, I am doing it to myself as well. Once that is fully understood, you would no sooner create a lack of food for another, than you would starve yourself.

I have noticed that currently, many of the children aren't always being taught to share. They are being taught to defend and to fear losing what they have, by parents who have been taught to fear everything too. If you look at the world you can see that clearly mirrored in our culture and world affairs. I hope the Mayans are right when they tell us that we are coming to a new beginning. It is always darkest before the dawn. It looks pretty dark outside in many pockets of the world. It may take some major global crisis to wake us up. When a crisis happens, people tend to put down their separateness and band together to help each other. Perhaps, the natural and man-made disasters around the globe are helping to bring us together, as one human family. When all else fails, disaster may be the cosmic *whack* that gets our attention.

Each one of us is walking a path that is unique to our individual SoulSelf. Most people are in various states of suffering, as the Buddha would call our present existence, without enlightenment. The need to feel special, important, valued, or included is the main agenda for the ego. We suffer when we feel lost, separate, devalued, etc. Peace and joy are not valued by the striving damaged ego. The pain body wants nothing to do with peace or joy of any kind although, it makes you believe that is exactly what you are striving for. The victim would not get the negative egoic mind fed, nor would the addict have any accuse for a fix, if happiness were to prevail in life.

A big question in the game we call life appears to be the relationship between ourselves and God. The Greatness of God is likely beyond our ability to conceive, let alone greatly impress. Some people spend their time trying to be so very important to God. Others feel that their God makes notes of all that we are doing on a daily basis, and judges us 'good or bad'. Some argue that none of this is real, and there is only God. There are those who have given up on the idea of a God entirely, and declare that human life is a random event in the universe. Many religions make 'demi' or 'mini' Gods to cover all the different aspects of life. Once we realize that we must be IN God/dess, the role of the creator becomes like the role of water to a fish. The water does not care in which direction the fish swims. Upstream or down is up to the fish.

I have heard us called Godlings. Could it be that being made in the image and likeness of God does not mean that God has a nose and mouth like we do? Maybe instead of looks, we are alike in attributes. We are creative beings in the micro, just as God is creative in the macro. Where our physical DNA originated from is irrelevant. Whether we are remembering some alien race that came down from the sky, or a father creator sitting in heaven, is missing the point. It is evident that something created us. That something created the animals, sky gods, the galaxies, the planets, and the quantum particles, that all the dense material stuff is made of. <u>That Great Something</u>, that first cause, whether it was done with a big bang or a small fizzle, had to create out of itself. Before there were two there had to be one. That is the true meaning of "we are all one". That "One" we need to call something and categorize it in our monkey mind. We generally call that Great Something 'God'. In our need to be right and feel safe, we have wars over the name of God, and the circumstances of God, and the most cherished of God. If you can get out of your little brain for a moment and look at the big picture, you will see that it is quite ludicrous to buy into any of these ideas of separation.

Just as a drop is to the ocean, we are a part of creation, at that level we are all ONE. We are part of that force, simply by the fact that we are in it. <u>It cannot be stated enough</u>, that there can be only one source, one power, and one presence, and we have to be in it. There is no possible way we can get out of *"All that IS"*. It is obvious that we are also creative beings, because we can move our energy, and create within our small place of existence. We can create a sentence, a book, a chair or a mess. We create by a law I call resonance. At this time, the 'Law of Attraction' is the buzz phrase. I am hesitant to use it here, as it doesn't quite fit my meaning. Yes, we use the law of attraction, to attract what resonates to our inner climate. It appears to me that many people are anesthetized by the phrase; "Oh yes, they say, "that's The law of attraction". They think they have the concept understood, and fail to take it to its deeper meaning. Resonating to something is done on the deepest level. You resonate to the ethnic culture you are born in, and you attract circumstances around that, until you develop the awareness that you can choose a different path.

Perhaps, we are trying to become more Godlike, and claim our own creations, instead of believing we are just experiencing random events. We have all heard the saying, "the apple doesn't fall far from the tree". This is the tree of life and we are children of God/dess. Owning your own creations means owning your God-self. God / Goddess / Life force / "All that IS", created everything, and you get to choose what to do with your portion of that energy. It is like your own personal can of cosmic play dough. We are Godlings playing in the denseness of the material world.

CHAPTER 11

The "Other Side"

T he bottom line is: I live in a meat suit in the land of duality. I believe I have chosen to be here at this time on Earth. I will surely not survive this. I will die and my soul will go somewhere. Is there an afterlife? I am a firm believer in reincarnation. If you're not, then perhaps you believe we only have one chance to get it right, and when we die, we will wait until judgment day in the duality of heaven and hell. If heaven is elsewhere, then where is this? Are we in hell? Is there suffering here? There certainly can be hell on Earth if we choose to experience it that way. Releasing our minds from hell is a good idea, no matter where it is or isn't.

It has been observed by countless subjects under hypnosis, while experiencing past life regression, that there is an afterlife. It appears to have an order and a purpose to it. To me the word afterlife is a misnomer. Life is eternal, and we are part of life. Perhaps, this is the dreamtime and life is really on the other side of the veil. Perhaps, life here on Earth is like looking in the mirror and believing that the reflection you see is the real you.

Near death experience are growing in awareness by the average person, due to television documentaries on the subject. It is also much more common to have someone speak of having a past life experience than it was 20 years ago. There are many documented cases of near death experiences. One of the glaringly evident things that come out of these experiences is a certainty, by those who experience them, that there is much more to life than living in a body. Once someone has had a near death experience (NDE), their priorities usually change and all the fuss about the little things of life are meaningless. It is often reported, that we go through some sort of tunnel and meet deceased loved ones when we leave our physical body. There is a grand reunion with those we have loved and lost. It is also often reported that someone who has harmed us is there seeking forgiveness, which is usually given willingly. Almost everyone has witnessed, or heard about, a loved one who is near death and appears to be talking to invisible others in the room. Quite often the others are dear to the person who is approaching death and have already crossed over into Spirit. The living relatives may not know who Gram is talking to as she passes, because they were not yet born while the other person was on the Earth plane.

NDE's either experienced or heard of from others, can help wake us up to the larger picture of who we are. For most of us, knowing that there is more than just this one lifetime is liberating. I would not want only one chance to get this right. What a relief to know that there is something beyond physical death. It is a blessing to learn that no matter how lost we get in addictions or any other negative behavior we can still be embraced by love when we leave this Earth. A near death experience expands our understanding of everything. We are seldom ever the same after this kind of experience. Having an NDE ensures that the lifetime will help us advance in our soul growth.

I will share my own experience about an elder dying and my own short NDE to help illustrate this concept.

Grandmothers crossing

I was called to NY from VA by my mother, to visit my 99 year old grandmother before she died. Grandmother and I were never close, because she was a very self-involved woman who had a clean fetish. You had to wash your hands, before you could touch her. *Not the cookie baking grandma to be sure.* I dutifully made the 7 hour trip to find this little old lady, who had not remembered who I was in years, lying near death in her bed. I walked into the room and this frail little old lady *sat up in bed*. She had not been able to sit up on her own for quite a while. She looked squarely at me and said, "Lorana, I knew you would come". Then she fell back on the bed and proceeded to tell me that she had suffered and how she wished she had known the suffering she had caused "that young man". I did not have a clue what she was talking about, but she seemed to need forgiveness. I told her she was certainly forgiven and she seemed relieved over that. She told me how frightened she was and how much she hurt. I placed my hands on her frail body and told her she would not be in pain where she was going. She settled into a peaceful sleep and was gone in 3 hours.

To me, this was evidence that family members are part of a group that you incarnate with. We have to play hide and seek to find our mates, but our family is a sure thing. On the other side of life, she and I must be much closer than we were here on the Earth plane.

My Out of Body NDE

In the 70's I had a NDE of my own. It was not as extensive as some of the reports I have read about, but it did change my life and now I am not afraid of death because of it. I was in the process of being electrocuted. While working in an old cosmetic factory, stringing thermostat wire above the drug counter I *accidently* touched a metal wire to a live 277 volt connection. I saw the fire flying out of my fingertips and my body suspended by the electricity flowing through it. I knew that if I touched the metal shelves in front of me it would be over and I could leave. I had stepped completely out of my body and I was a witness to what was happening. I could feel a loving presence near me and knew everything was going to be fine. I got the idea that I could choose to leave or stay. I was enveloped in a sensation that can only be called love, but that word does not really express what it was like. It was tantalizing to consider leaving, as I casually pondered the possibility for a moment. When I thought of my young children, leaving became much less appealing and I chose to stay. I then surveyed the situation and in my 'oh so cosmic' voice I heard myself say... "Step off the ladder Stupid". I fell about 6 ft. into an open box of 'Charmin' toilet tissue which was thankfully, 'squeezably soft'.

I was in shock and had electric burns, but other than that I was unharmed. What struck me as the most amazing part of the experience was the lack of emotion such as anguish, fear, or worry that I felt while witnessing the event. There was also no great desire or longing to stay because everything was just 'the way it was'. From that experience I understood that emotion is only felt while here on Earth and are what fuel our desires and addictions. They are the main ingredient we use, when we are using the law of attraction.

Mediumship

Another means of getting validation about life beyond death is through Mediumship. Spiritualism is a religion founded on the premise that those in the spirit world can communicate with us through a medium. Television is airing many shows about Psychic Mediums who talk to the dead. Usually the messages are simple ones that validate the departed loved ones continuing existence and that their love for the person who is receiving the message lives on. Speaking from my experiences of 'talking to the dead' I arrived at some of my own conclusions regarding the spirit world. I have become aware that "just because you are dead does not mean you are smart". Some souls don't appear to have a much greater awareness when they are dead, than they did while alive. I have witnessed Spiritual entities that are still very attached to the physical side of life. In the case of addiction, especially to alcohol, it is suggested by various Mediums that those souls are drawn to places such as taverns where they can still be close to their old habit. I personally believe that you can choose to sever that connection on either side of the veil once you can heal the cause of the behavior. There are likely some young souls who have not yet learned that the physical world of possessions and events are simply tools for advancement. They still want to affect things on this side of the veil. I suspect that this results in ghosts and hauntings. I do not align my energy with this kind of phenomenon because, I don't care to play with ghosts and goblins. I do not condone bad behavior in children on either side of the veil. Long ago I imagined that when a person died they automatically became holy spiritual beings, with nothing but love to give. I have since learned that life on both sides of the veil of birth and death is a process of awakening.

CHAPTER 12

Life in the Spirit World

There is a new therapy called Life between Lives, commonly referred to as LBL. In this therapy the client is taken into the death experience in a past life regression, and then asked to go on and report what the afterlife is like. It is reasoned that learning what our soul's purpose was when incarnating heals problems once we are deep within them. There are now hundreds of practitioners trained in this technique and they all report basically the same thing. We feel deep remorse in our shortcomings and joy in our successes once we cross over. According to LBL sessions, we feel every good thing and mean thing we have done as if we were the person that we harmed or helped. This takes the golden rule of "Do unto others as you would have them do unto you" to a whole new level. Our every action is recorded in our own subconscious mind and played back for review, after we cross over into the spirit world. In our life review, our own meanness can feel like we are in a hell of our own making and what we perceive as small kindness carry great rewards. A panel of elders and guides are available to help and assist, but not to condemn or punish. It is easier for many to believe that we are mere puppets and there is a higher power that has our plan in hand and will make us behave. Self-responsibility is frightening. Hence, again I say, *"Young Soul Planet"*. It is just like a 4 year old on his way to school for the first time. He wants to be a big kid, but he doesn't want to leave his Mom... Young children and young souls usually test their boundaries.

Total awareness and enlightenment is the ultimate goal and does not happen just because we leave one of our physical vehicles. LBL reports that after a difficult lifetime, in most cases, healing and a complete forgiveness of SoulSelf is achieved with the help of our Spirit guides. Once achieved, the desire to begin planning another lifetime wells up in the soul. Ultimately, we begin the process of choosing another lifetime, because we desire to bring balance to our experiences, thereby advancing our soul. Perhaps, we will accept a difficult rebirth as atonement for a previous lifetime that was way off the mark. Eastern religion calls this balancing Karma. Our master guides and teachers will help us with our choices. Not all difficulties are punishment; they are opportunities for us to change our life path. In LBL sessions it has been reported that occasionally a soul is so damaged that it cannot be healed in the Spirit world after a very difficult lifetime and very poor choices. Higher beings can decide that it must be "recycled". It is something like being totally cleansed and made ready to begin again.

Once we are ready to reincarnate, the parents and the era of time are selected. Then the SoulSelf is able to step into the scene and try on events that are being planned with the other characters in their personal screen play. It sounds like dress rehearsal doesn't it? LBL, sessions report that we never have all of our energy here. Part of us always remains in Spirit. That makes me think that my "Higher Self" is the part I left behind. It might be more correct to say, I am the project that my Higher Self is working on.

It has also been reported by LBL subjects, that we are part of larger soul groups. These are souls who are in a form of class together, and who are learning from and with each other. Your soul mates are usually around you in your lifetime. There are also master guides and Archangels who watch the happenings, and step in if it's necessary. It is certain that some of the key players in your life are part of your soul group. The *'chance'* meetings with them are influential in your journey here on Earth. I often get the question, "is he my soul mate"? If you have been married for 20 years it's likely you had connections in other lifetimes. Soul-mates know where all your buttons are, and it is their duty to push them at appropriate times. It might be better to ask if he is the "nice sweet soul mate" that you are wishing for. Probably not so much…If he is, count your blessings. If he isn't, you can count them anyway. You get the opportunity to dance together with Grace, loving or leaving each other in this lifetime, with honor and blessings. LBL reports describe soul groups in school together on the "other side", but apparently the strongest lessons come while we are incarnated. While in the physical, it is easier to acquire merit than it is when we know the game, but can't play it. Which is what happens, without the *land of forgetting*, that we experience while here on Earth.

My point is that here on Earth, in any life choice, you can choose joy over suffering, peace over war... acceptance over resistance. In the land of duality you can choose either side at any time. Everybody has problems and lessons to be learned and the theater we choose to learn those lessons in is created with purpose and is chosen by us. There can be as much pain in having as not having. Happiness does not come from outer circumstances, but rather from inner circumstances. Here on Earth, duality is the illusion that runs the planet. There is nothing here that is not part of that duality. Peace/War, Joy/Suffering... It is in your choosing that you grow. You set the stage and you pick the actors. In the case of a very young soul, there is a lot of help from their friends, both here and in Spirit.

Participating in an LBL session is a very rewarding experience for those that can achieve it. To understand why we have chosen our partners and experiences is healing. Large numbers of these case studies have been published by Michael Newton in his series called * "Journey of Souls", if you would care to explore this subject further.

CHAPTER 13

Choosing Lifetimes

Life Screen Dream

I had a dream about my decision to come here... I know that seems strange to some, but you should be used to *'strange'* in my life by now. I certainly am. Dreams can be memories, or messages from Spirit.

I was standing in a great marble hall before a device that I could touch and make events change on its screen. This was many years ago, before personal computers were introduced, let alone touch screens. I had been working on a big contract or scheme of some kind. I was so happy to have my plan finished. Papers and charts came out of the machine, which I grabbed and then excitedly ran outside. I descended long marble steps into a throng of hooded figures and milling people. I was impatient to get on with my journey, so I ran past them and jumped off what seemed like a subway platform. As I was sinking into the darkness, I realized that I had left someone behind. I am not sure who it was that I left behind.

When my third child was born he looked at me with complete recognition. I was struck with the idea, that he and I had known each other in many lifetimes. I wonder if he was the one I did not wait for? I met my soul twin late in life and he was 10 years younger than I. Perhaps things would have been different had I waited for him?? I am sure I will know when I next cross over. To this day patience is a lesson for me.

The charts I had in my hand reminded me of astrology charts. I became a certified astrologer early in this life. Recognizing the chart I had seen in my dream helped me find one of my life paths. Many years later, as I was thumbing through a book by a famous psychic, I saw a drawing, almost exactly like the machine I was standing in front of in my dream. I also saw the stairs I went down, and the big courtyard I went into, drawn from her visions.

I often wonder if this isn't all a dream, and I am astral traveling back to real LIFE on the other side at night while I am sleeping. Since we are immortal beings having a human experience, the answer must be 'Both'. Whether reality is here or elsewhere does not matter as much as what we choose to do while we are in our living dream.

To be born into flesh we must merge with a body and a mind. This body and mind is grown from an existing pair of body/minds that are in the midst of experiencing life in the physical. Before we arrive, we have chosen our parents, and the life circumstances that we will arrive in. Before we incarnate, our life path is mapped out <u>by</u> us, not for us. How we find our way through our life path once we get here is the essence of the game of life. We are not the body we are moving into, any more than we are the car that we drive. Just as a car does not drive by itself, a body does not survive without a soul enlivening it.

The mechanics of the physical body are in place upon conception, but the soul's choice to inhabit it is only tentative at first. Our body vehicle is not totally agreed to by our soul until later in the process of gestation. It is much like a warrantee, if the linkup between our soul and our physical being does not mesh correctly, either side can "opt out". Both sides have a buyer's clause of sorts. I tell my clients often that there is no need to carry guilt around for the rest of their life, because they had a miscarriage or decided to terminate a pregnancy. I believe that often the same soul comes back to you at a more appropriate time. I would also like to say that indiscriminate unprotected sex when you are not trying to have a child is irresponsible. Young souls must learn responsibility.

Our SoulSelf, which is part of our OverSoul, merges with the body/mind created for us by our parents. Through the marriage of the body/mind, with the Spirit or SoulSelf, we setup our life, and our personal realities. Body, Mind and Spirit are the trinity of our physical being. Once our journey has begun, it is up to us to learn to choose consciously. I tell people all the time that they are 'in their right place by right of their consciousness'. Most of the time, they look at me like I am a crazy woman when I say that. Once they understand the full impact of that statement, they are on their way to choosing their experiences consciously.

When we get here, we have an agenda that we would like to complete with as much Grace as possible. We know before we get here, that we must attract circumstances, people and events into our lives that will fulfill our plan. We also know that we will forget our plan once we are totally immersed in the denseness of 3d reality. I call our intended plan a soul contract. Having your astrology chart done can help you understand your intended path, but not the particular circumstances of it. Astrology is not the only way to understand the energy available to you when you incarnate, but it can be very helpful to those interested in the subject. Astrology is far too vast a subject for this book, but you can find many books that will help you decipher your astrology chart. We are said to have free will. I say that we have free will within the scope of our soul contract. We certainly have the free will to screw things up, if we get lost in the illusion and don't respond to our well planned clues. I guess we could then be classified as 'lost souls'. Guess who is looking for us... WE are...

'Clues' are life happenings that bump us along our chosen path, even though we may not be aware of it. It also appears that even when we veer off the path there are detour signs that get us back to our designated points of importance. Our personal guides are always there to help us along with gentle reminders in the form of chance, hunches and nudges. Sometimes it takes a good cosmic *whack* to get our attention if we are exceptionally lost. Accidents are good course trajectory correctors when nothing else works. Once we learn to pay more attention to our inner guidance, life gets easier to manage...

Why we are here, and what we are to do about it, takes up a lot of our attention on Earth, even if we don't consciously see it that way. The force that we come from is creative, and I know for sure that we are creative also. It has been proven that in the quantum world we actually affect our circumstances with the mental pictures we create. The first time I learned of the 'particle theory' and quantum physics, I instantly equated it to how our mind affects our reality. We can create a masterpiece or a mess; it is up to us. Perhaps it is the act of creating, more than the outcome of our creation that satisfies the universal creative desire. No one can know why God created in the first place, but we can use our part of that creative power to make our personal piece of the cosmos a joyful place or a hell on earth. It's our choice.

When I tell someone that they picked their parents and their social status, before they came to Earth, it usually doesn't go over very well. On the surface this is a pretty radical statement. How could someone choose to be born in poverty, intolerance, illness, abuse, neglect, violence etc.? On the other side of the coin, it would seem that choosing to be born into wealth and a loving family, would be desirable, and a just reward. If that is always true then, what about the danger of slipping into vanity or greed? Those characteristics usually bring much suffering with them too.

It is only when we can see how we have grown, because of our life choices that things become a bit easier to accept. I also tell my clients that our parents are responsible for our *first wound,* which is the very thing that the entire incarnation is all about fixing. For instance, in the land of duality, how would you know that you wanted to grow in the art of forgiveness, if you had nothing to forgive? If you have chosen an average family with loving parents, pat yourself on the back, and then look deeper for the wounding, or look elsewhere. If you picked a dysfunctional family, you don't have to look very far for what you came to work on. . I call it an *accelerated learning class.*

We are learning that we create, or attract our own reality. We create in our personal life, by using the same power that we are created with. When we first begin to understand that we create every circumstance in our life, and that accidents don't happen as often as planned events, it is pretty frightening. I remember when this concept first came to me. I was afraid that I would fail at Science of Mind if I got sick or something bad happened to me. The weight of the responsibility to demonstrate a successful and healthy life was almost crushing. It took me years to really embrace the idea that I needed to accept my chosen experiences as valuable. Acceptance of 'what is' includes the fallibility of my physical body. It was when I began to get information about the life contract that things made more sense. We may have included illness or accidents to help balance past actions or just to get our own attention. It can't be stated enough that when we are unaware of our SoulSelf, a good jolt of bad karma can cause a transformation of Spirit.

The search for the sacred begins in times of trouble, and usually help arrives, and some good comes of it. How many times have you looked back and said, "I hated that at the time, but it turned out to be the best thing that ever happened to me"? Oftentimes, when there is a crisis, the local clergy is quick to step in, and offer comfort from their brand of God. Sadly, I have witnessed harm coming from a zealot who was using others suffering to further his own agenda. He was condemning, shaming, and blaming the person he was ministering to…Of course on some level that particular cleric was attracted to further the purpose of his parishioner. More often than not, a minister has the best of intentions and helps us touch the sacred space inside us where healing can begin. In truth, we will always be in touch with the sacred, because it is within our own hearts. As we mature, there will come a time when crisis is unnecessary to jolt us out of our stupor, while we are in the physical world

Therefore, the bottom line is that I have chosen to be here on Earth. I am perhaps part Alien and part primate, made from within something much greater than either. I, nonetheless, have to do something with all this and take part in the game. Why? I don't know, but I must have had a plan or I would not have chosen to come and play. As I said, I totally believe in other lifetimes, yet I strive to do this one the best I can. An old friend use to say, "This is the life you're dying to live". In the end, I would like to present my SoulSelf, with its collected experiences and the appropriate healing to the Spirit of the ONE, "All that IS", God. I don't know if there is an end, but it sounds good. A lofty goal, wouldn't you say?

CHAPTER 14

Time

Time is a key element in keeping things in order in 3d reality. We believe that the law of time is immutable, but it is not. What would happen if time changed its properties and acted differently? Scientists are now talking about time in a different way. Time is a measurement of events in space. We now have a new measurement called, space time. This theory was first presented by Albert Einstein, and is now being proven by modern science. Time appears to bend and warp. It comes in units like time slots. Many philosophers and scientists are saying that time is speeding up. It is theorized that it is because we are at the top of the egg of our long cycle through the cosmos, as we move into our new age. We could be coming to the top of our curve, OR moving into a New

World Age. What is spectacular about our current cycle is that both events are happening at once. My theory is that as the curve of time gets sharper, *it takes less time to make time.* It is also being reported that the wobble of our axis is narrowing and slowing down. Airports have had to adjust their radar to compensate for the changes in our wobble and the shifting of magnetic north which is said to be due to the changing wobble.

I am sure there is much more to it than I can possibly describe with my scientifically challenged brain, but this is how I have made sense of it all. I imagine driving down a road that has a big long curve in it. At first the curve is gradual then suddenly it makes a sharp bend. You have to break and then accelerate in order to maneuver the curve safely. Perhaps, the breaking has something to do with the smaller wobble of our axis and then the sensation of time speeding up is related to the acceleration. I believe it's helpful to be able to understand what is happening in simple enough terms so that we won't totally panic if things change quickly or time stands still.

I can only experience reality through my own perceptions, and to me it seems like time *is* moving faster. It may be the power of suggestion, but now 8 hours go by in what seems like only 4. I believe that the way we experience time is changing. Perhaps time will stop and everything will be happening at once. If that were the case, the moment you thought of something it would materialize. I have heard that acid trips were like that. It might be that when the brain is released from the constraints of physical reality by a chemical, it loses it's time line.

I don't believe that the world is ending, but time as we know it, might be. If that is the case we will all experience the astral plane, where everything does happen at once. It may be only for a little while, but we won't be able to understand that while it is happening. A little while in the cosmos could mean centuries, by our current measurements, before the orbit elongates again. The way time stretches could change permanently.

If duality is an illusion, then time may well be part of that illusion, or even what facilitates it. I have read from various sources over the years that our OverSoul came here to play in physical reality and got caught in it. If that is true, then it might be time that caught us. We might now be seeing, not just a window of time, but also our escape route. That may be why many of the 'new age' people feel the urgency to wake up and shift out of this dimension. We may be graduating, or we may need to escape, but needing to move on seems to be the key. I suspect that the delicious physical experiences of emotion and passion had a lot to do with our wanting to come and play here in the first place. The problem is that it loses its luster over time. (Pardon the pun) I believe that once we got involved with physical reality, there was no turning back. Now we must bring the physical being into spiritual awareness.

We are creative beings having a human experience and time is what we use to measure that experience. Life can be seen as a game that is sometimes not much fun, but terribly addictive. In the Game of Life, we create things and events with our mind, by using the laws of attraction, and believe we have to wait for time to pass before we can have them. When we are using our creative energy the secret is that we have to ignore time. We must pretend that it doesn't exist and that our desire is available in the present moment. The present moment is where the power is, because the present moment is actually all there is. Outside of time everything is happening at once. Magic and miracles happen outside of the confines of time. It is now obvious that we are creative beings in our personal world. That means we have the power to create events, circumstances, and things in our lives. We only have the power to do that NOW, because Now is all that really exists.

Buying into the concept of time means you have to wait for what you want. Waiting is an illusion. The trick to manifesting our desires in this denseness is to know that time doesn't really exist, except as a tool to keep us from bumping into our future and our past. We have to *expect* our desire to become reality, because of the fact that we are creative beings. At the same instant, we must be grateful for what we have brought into existence, even if we won't be able to see it for a space of time. It is not because it doesn't already exist, but because of the time delay in our current situation. The great teacher Jesus taught us in Mark 11:24. *"Therefore I say to you, all things for which you pray and ask, believe that you have received them, and they will be granted you"*. You are to pray as if you have already received. Without having to wait in time, that becomes a fact. The minute we create it, it is done.

Slinky of Time

I was taught by Simon Peter, that time is not linear, and lifetimes do not have to cohere to time lines. We can play in the sandbox of time any place we choose. Imagine that a slinky is stretched out on a table, and anchored to a board at both ends. Every swirl of the slinky represents a measure of time. Up-end the board and you will have a model of how time works. When you think about time all happening at once, you can picture the slinky. It only seems long, but it is really piled on top of itself.

You can choose to come into the time game at any place that works best for you. Some people have experienced what they call their future selves. Your last lifetime could have been in the year 2420. There are hypnotherapists who offer future life progressions, which are possible because of all time being 'Now'. There are those who reason that if this is true, then everything that can happen has already happened and there is nothing that can change it. Perhaps that is true, and every possibility has already been thought into existence in time. We would still have to use these events to learn and grow. Mathematics already existed before you learned about it in grade school. Since we are creative beings, we may be able to add a new slant to some old event in time. 2+2 could end up equaling z.

CHAPTER 15

Ascension

There is a large group of individuals who believe this era is the time of the **ascension**. It is a time when we take our bodies with us and rise into a higher plane of existence. They believe that just as Jesus ascended to heaven, we will be going somewhere "up there" too. It might also be a case of "beam me up Scottie". In the future, we might be dropping the illusion of time and the denseness of the 3D reality. We could then begin to live as *soul entities*. We would release the need to be reborn and perhaps, move to a different dimension. The Mayans say that we are moving into the 5th age from the 4th age. It is easy to equate this to shifting into the 5th dimension, which agrees with the ascension theory. Some say that in the 5th dimension we will not need a physical body as we know it. There are others who say we will take our place with our star brothers and travel to other galaxies, as well as be able to shift dimensions. I vote for that scenario! If I am to take a body with me as I ascend into the next plane, I would like to choose a taller one that is lighter weight.

Most concur that by any means available; we are jumping off the wheel of birth and death. We are leaving this valley of illusion called life, and transcending the need for duality. This is the goal and reward of enlightenment. On the other hand, perhaps none of this is true and we are no better than cockroaches living on the mother Goddess. We are afraid of losing our happy home to floods, earthquakes and disasters. Since I really don't like that scenario, I prefer to think it is our Graduation. I believe that by the proper climate of our collective mind, we will have placed our currency of attention into the basket of love and brotherhood, joy and happiness, and we will be moving on to the next great adventure. If we dwell in fear and hate while the Earth is shaking, and our way of life is changing, then perhaps we will have to repeat the class elsewhere.

Ascension dream

The only vision I have had about ascension was a very powerful one.

I was walking with a very large group of people across rolling hills and valleys. I was dressed as a shepherd. Nobody seemed to know where they were going, and the others seemed to be following me. That made me uncomfortable, because I didn't know where I was going either. We crested a hill and saw that the valley was filled with throngs of people. Everything was calm and peaceful, even though there were thousands of people standing and sitting on the ground. I instinctively knew that this was where I was supposed to be. Down from the sky, a wooden dock was lowered with a man standing on it. He was dressed in a brown sack cloth and had stringy hair that covered his face. I could see his rope sandals very clearly. Even though he was far away, it seemed as if he was right in front of me and he was as big as a giant. A rope was suspended from somewhere above the clouds and it was coiled on the deck. This rope was as big as an ocean liner rope and when he pulled it he had to bend way over and use all his upper body strength. He pulled the rope and a bell tolled that was so loud it vibrated the ground.

The bell rang and a number of people simply disappeared. There was a rustling in the crowd, but no one panicked. There wasn't a body left and no one saw them leave. The bell tolled again and again people disappeared. I began to understand that they were being transported to somewhere else. The bell tolled for the third time, and again people disappeared. I was becoming concerned that I would not be taken. With that thought I believe I conveyed a willingness to go. When the bell tolled again, I felt the most vivid sensation of being turned inside out from my feet to my head. It was an indescribable, but totally joyous feeling. At that moment I found myself STANDING straight up in my bed. My partner was sleeping next to me, and was undisturbed.

I don't think I have been the same since. That dream was in 1991. If there is ascension, I am reasonably sure that the feeling I had is what it would be like.

CHAPTER 16

Mayan Calendar

The Mayan Calendar ended on Dec 21, 2012 and just as Jan 1, 2000 was foretold as doomsday so too was 2012. Let us take a look at what the Mayans say about all of this. If we believe that the world is going to end, then I guess there is no point in worrying about any of our problems. Drink up, shoot up, charge or stuff yourself with sweets, because none of it matters, the sky is falling. On the other hand, since we are here after Dec 21, 2012, perhaps we should think about how to fix the mess we have made of this planet and ourselves.

I recently revisited the Mayan ruins of Chichen Itzu in the Yucatan. I was also there in the mid 80's, and the difference today is astounding. I was able to climb the great pyramid in the 80's, and the grounds were open for us to explore in their beautiful, natural setting. On this visit, I could only take pictures of the pyramid, and could not even get into the ball court, let alone hear someone speak clearly, from all the way across the massive court. This visit was a shopping experience. Our world has moved from beauty to commerce. The street vendors were all along the path we were to walk. It has become a bazaar. It made me think of the story of Jesus, and the money changers in the temple. How like the condition of our society today, the poor line the streets of the cities peddling what they can to survive, while those on top can't be reached.

Our Mayan tour guide first explained that the Mayans did not mysteriously disappear. They are still in Mexico being tour guides. Then he explained that the Mayan calendar stops at 12/21/2012 because, that is the beginning of a new age, and the end of the old one.

Mayans view time differently than we do. Their calendars measure huge spans of time. We have small one year calendars and are focused on days and months, while theirs measures ages. They see time as a measurement of energy that charts the heavens from the standpoint of 5200 year cycles. We are moving from the Piscean age into the Aquarian age. Ages are blocks of time that describe the climate of human consciousness that is experienced during the different cycles. As the Piscean age is leaving, the effects of its ruling planet Neptune are beginning to wane. Neptune rules creative imagination and illusion, which are now rushing in for a last hurrah. We have taken our creative energy into the computer age and we have taken our illusion to the plague of addiction that appears on this planet now. Coming in is an age of human compassion and tolerance of all beings. Aquarius will meld technology with humanity in new and innovative ways.

Mayan Reset Button

Isn't it interesting, that the "New Age-ers" are all about healing and brotherhood, and the new zodiac sign we are heading into is Aquarius, which is the sign of the **brotherhood of man**. In the 60's the song was ♫ "This is the Dawning of the Age of Aquarius" ♫. The words to that song tell the story of what Aquarius is all about. It really sounds like a good thing to me. I am excited to have a new beginning. Did I mention that I am Aquarius? The 60's are coming into their own, because those who brought in the dawning in the 60's are now <u>in</u> their 60's.

The Mayans teach us that we are coming to the end of a complete cycle of time called a Long Count. This is a 144,000 year cycle of time, which represents the time it takes for the entire solar system to revolve through the ages. We are approaching our ecliptic. Translated, that means that our revolution as a solar system, around what all the other solar systems are revolving around, has come to the top of its egg shaped orbit. At this point we are farthest away from the center, and lined up like the sites on a rifle, dead center to the *center of the center* of the galaxies. I am sure that this simplified version is not what an astronomer would give you, but this is what makes sense to me.

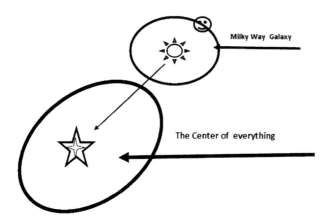

Being at our farthest point from Galactic center, you could say that we are as far from home as we can get. We feel lost and alone when we are so far from our center. Just like the winter solstice of Dec. 21, we are experiencing the longest night and the rebirth of the Sun. We are told that the energy gets darker, at this time. It was written by the ancients, that it will get so dark and dense that we even forget who we really are. It certainly seems like we have forgotten something, doesn't it? War, separation, and inequality are good indicators of our current social forgetfulness.

This cycle has happened before and reflects the cycles of the Earth changes that are taking place on the planet now. It is expected that we will have global weather shifts, great ice ages, and melting. Here again we see the destruction, followed by renewal. Those who came before us survived to tell us about it, and we will too. We are feeling a loss of connection, both spiritually and emotionally, to the Earth and to each other. Many of our religions see demons and devils coming at us, while others see angels coming to save us---of course only if we are worthy. What is really taking place is transformation.

Perhaps, the Earth simply shifts her land mass every million years or so, to let some parts of her skin rest and others take a turn blossoming for a new crop of young souls. Every good farmer knows that they have to cycle their crops. They have to let some fields go fallow every few years, or the crops will not grow in them. It might be that the Earth changes actually allow some of the land mass to rest, while others are uncovered and made ready for use. Perhaps Gaia is a good farmer too. We can accept what is happening on Earth with great anticipation, or we can wait in fear for doom. I choose to accept what will be and stay centered in the knowledge that I am safe in the process of life. I believe that I chose to be here, and that no matter what happens, **I am an immortal soul.**

Vision of two Earths

I would like to share a vision I had over 30 years ago which seems to relate to the Earth Changes and the coming age… I was standing in space looking at the Earth. I marveled at how fast it appeared to be traveling. All at once, it hit something, later portrayed by Star trek as, a 'plasma shield'. It split into two Earths of the same size. After it hit this membrane and split, one angled down, and one angled up. The one going down was lush, dense, and green. The one that went up was still green and looked the same, only less dense, and it was hazy. It looked lighter in weight, but not in size. I knew I wanted to go with the lighter one, even though the greener denser one was exquisitely beautiful.

Perhaps, there will be such a choice to make. Please understand that one was not better than the other. I was just witnessing the event. I wonder if we are coming to that plasma shield now. Will we be able to choose which Earth we will go with? Do all of us have to go the same way?

Examining Beliefs

CHAPTER 17

Religious Dogma

In order to move forward and heal our society, it is important to understand what we have taken into our belief system by default. Our religions give us an understanding of the way things are and how we fit into the overall scheme of life. Often they are absorbed by us when we are children and go unquestioned for decades. Guilt, blame and shame are used by many religious traditions to keep their parishioners in line. Guilt, blame and shame are also the root causes for most addictive behavior. It is an important part of healing and soul growth to examine what you believe and how you arrived at your beliefs. It is also very important to apply some logic and reason to your beliefs. Blind faith may not be the answer in the coming AGE. I am not going to elaborate on all the world religions, but I would like to give you my understanding of the overall flavor of the ones I am familiar with.... Suffice to say that most of them have ascended masters, virgin births, and other miracles.

I am not a follower of any particular religion. I primarily, use the New Testament and Buddhism in my Science of Mind ministry, simply because that is what most of the people I see are familiar with. My ministry is not about, "who had it right". It is about how we can heal our lives, our country, and our planet. I would rather see good results, than argue about causes.

Many people are still looking for a book of rules to follow, so they can do things in a certain way, to insure their safety and be "saved". The core 'truths' have become polluted. It appears that the current sets of rules are not working anymore. It does not appear to matter which tradition you follow, because there is a lack of spiritual values all over the globe. "This is a young soul planet" and young souls would react just like young children, to the type of chaos they have created in the world. They would try to control their environment, or try to ignore the problem. If that failed, they would act out in irrational and destructive ways.

What is important, are the severe results of needing to validate the dogma associated with one brand of religion over another. If you need to believe in something, but it has no concrete proof, you create a need to have it validated by others. By doing this you make it more believable to yourself. Where it gets dangerous is when one group feels the need to kill those who don't believe in the same way that they do. If we are to heal our social ills, we will have to address the affect that religion has had on what different people see as the duality of right and wrong. Having at least a basic knowledge of the flavor of what the major religions are teaching their followers is important when trying to understand and peacefully co-exist with our fellow humans.

The ultimate example of duality and childishness on this young soul planet is, "MY God is better than your God". This is basically the same as 'My Father is richer than your Father... My Dad can beat up your Dad'... That sounds like schoolyard antics, doesn't it? Young souls need parents to make them feel safe and Father Gods in heaven are all they can find to do the job.

In the United States, where Christianity has been the primarily excepted "truth", we are taught that we are born sinful and we need the pastor or the priest to help save us. Salvation is an ongoing struggle and you must be ever vigilant, lest you transgress. Somehow putting money in the collection plate will make you safe from hell. The clergy that condemns us also has the antidote for our troubles. How convenient, this makes great job security.

I am not promoting any one religion over another. A dear friend of mine calls religion by two names, there is political religion and Spiritual religion. Political religion has an agenda that has little to do with helping anyone. It is geared toward crowd control. I find political religion illogical at best and harmful at worst. I believe that it is important to create sacred space, but that space is between you and your creator, which is Spiritual religion. Religion is often an attempt by young souls, to find a God or Goddess that they think is outside of them. Because young souls can be rather self-centered, they have attempted to create God in their own image.

There is good in religions, because they all serve their purpose in some areas of life, especially for young souls. Christians teach us to surrender to God, or Let go and Let God. I often hear people say "It's in the Lords hands". I believe that it is high wisdom to "turn it over" to the Lord in times of trouble. When you are hurting and can't be objective or abstract about the mechanics of the universal law of attraction, turning it over to God works very well. Having a Spiritual community and feeling like a part of a larger purpose is comforting. If you just turn everything over to the Lord without even trying to take the reins of your life, you are actually living by default. You can blame the bad things on God or on yourself for doing something to displease God. With maturity comes responsibility. We begin to understand that we have a hand in shaping our own curriculum.

Having no religion or belief in anything other than randomness seems difficult to me. Having no God must be more comforting to some people than thinking someone is watching their every move and judging them harshly. Much of society is still unaware of any Spiritual truth, other than the dogma learned from their church. A large number of people are so frightened by what they learned in church, that they don't go near the place if they can avoid it. What they did get, and are frightened of, is that they are born wrong, and will be going to hell for it. Many of my clients do not even want to hear the word God or Jesus due to their past experiences with religion. I know that many recovering alcoholics turn to Jesus as their higher power, and it works for them. I also know of many that will not attend a twelve step group because of all the Jesus talk. I believe that once someone is able to put religion in the right perspective in their mind, they can use it to help themselves grow.

A vast number of people go about their lives in fear and victimization, or righteous indignation. Others are so caught up in trying to find their next meal or paying the massive debt for the stuff that they think defines them, they have no time to even ponder any deeper questions. Many believe that we are going into Armageddon, the end of the world is coming, and there are no options. Sadly, leaders of countries feel that it is their duty to ride the horses into Armageddon or Jihad for the glory of their brand of God. Christianity teaches that God is coming back and he will judge us, keep 144,000 and make the rest suffer. I heard a Texan friend make this profound statement. In his deep Texas drawl he said, "It can't be only 144,000 that are going to get into heaven, because there are more Baptist preachers in Texas than that"! The number 144,000 may well be the amount of years it takes to circle the ages, instead of the number of "*goodly souls*" of Christendom that will be saved.

I don't mean to be trite, but these ideas are so illogical. Why would we be given a brain to reason with and then be asked to put reasoning aside and believe in some dogma that doesn't even make sense? We are told to go on blind faith about what the clergy has interpreted that God meant to say. We are told in Genesis that it was wrong for Adam to eat from the tree of knowledge. It was obviously preferable to keep us in ignorance. When he did eat the fruit of knowledge he was kicked out of the garden and of course it was blamed on the woman. Who do you think might have written that, REALLY? Humans have been bending scripture to fit their own agenda for a very long time. In this case, ask yourself who had an agenda that suppressed women, and wanted to keep them in ignorance? If it was Gods will that women were supposed to be subordinate, why are they smart and able to talk? Wouldn't God, in *his* infinite wisdom have made women mute? I would think that if the creator of the Universe wanted us to know something we would all hear it loud and clear. It doesn't seem like God would need *some guy from the church* to speak on God's behalf.

Stop and think about how large the entire cosmos is and how many planets and stars there are. Now realize that you are on one tiny planet in the Milky Way galaxy. The percentage of probability that we are not the only planet that supports life is better than 95%. Isn't it preposterous to believe that we can anger the God that made all of creation, because we said a bad word, or took a shine to a neighbor's wife, or showed too much cleavage? Have you ever wondered why there is so much emphasis placed on sexual conduct? While it is very true, that certain kinds of conduct might not be acceptable in the society you live in, it likely misses the attention of the creator of the Universe. Religions made sexual energy wrong, and when they did they created a "no win situation" for their followers. Did they need their followers to feel guilt so they can sell absolution?

With the idea of Alien influence in mind, any good horse breeder knows that it is not good to pollute the gene pool. They want the toughest stallions, and the most submissive mares. If we did have some interference from space beings tampering with our DNA, I could see where they would not have wanted us having our way, with whomever we chose, and polluting the experiment. In the Sumerian cuneiform writing and in biblical literature, it sounded like there was also a problem with the Gods just throwing their seed anywhere they wanted, down here among the "daughters of men". That may be why our subconscious thinks it's so important to divide the races. I would hope those days are over, and now moral behavior is only important for good mental health. Sadly, with few exceptions, that does not appear to be the case. Countries were founded on the rules of sexual conduct. Government offices are won or lost over sexual conduct instead of intelligence. It's still very much a man's world.

Healthy self-respect regarding sexuality is important in how you feel about yourself. Self-esteem is one of the keys to a balanced and healthy life. If you feel bad about yourself, then some part of creation feels bad. It is a cancer cell in the Spiritual body of the OverSoul. We want to feel good about ourselves, so we tell ourselves stories about what good is. The problem is that our stories came from fables that are impossible to achieve. There are also many people who believe that suffering will get them a high place in heaven. Others believe life is so full of suffering that they have to get "High" to find heaven. Many try to avoid the deep pain and grief they feel by masking or drowning it with addictive substances and behaviors. It is because they feel like frightened and powerless children who have been abandoned by an absent God.

*"A Course in Miracles" teaches that everyone feels guilty, because they bought into the idea of being separate from God in the first place. That belief was a form of betrayal for which we subconsciously punish ourselves. Maybe, we are ashamed that we got caught in the time bubble and are trapped here. I think it is more important to look at where we are, instead of spending time trying to figure out, how we got to where we are. It is time to embrace the fact that we are all part of one Spirit... When we do that we will let go of the past, stop condemning ourselves, and start really loving and accepting

ourselves. When we realize that the physical body is our vehicle not who we are, dogma ceases to make any sense at all. Perhaps, the changes we are seeing in the world are bringing the light of wisdom with them. Perhaps, the lights will come on, and we will become "enlightened". If the lights are on and someone is home the religious dogma that doesn't make sense will come under the scrutiny of conscious and aware people. We will be able to keep the best and trash the rest.

CHAPTER 18

Jesus the Rabbi

Jesus was an enlightened master who understood who he was. He knew that he was made of God-stuff. He was teaching others who they were also. He performed miracles, and told his students that they too could perform miracles. All they had to do was believe it. Christianity was born after his death. His name was not Jesus Christ. His name was Jesus of Nazareth. The word Christ means messiah, deliverer, or savior. Jesus was a Rabbi who was teaching the basic oneness of God.

The Jewish faith puts God in the center of everything. It teaches that God is the creator of the Universe and "All that IS" in it. The Jewish people were expecting a Messiah to deliver them from bondage. Because of Jesus's apparent Spiritual strength, some of the people decided that he would fit into the slot as the ONE. Very little is known about Jesus's life from around age 7 to when he was 30. I am sure he displayed extraordinary Spiritual talents throughout his life.

The Jewish people believed that someone was going to be born a king and bring them the law of God again. This king was also supposed to save them from their oppressors and give them back their rights and property. The leaders of the temple were under pressure to produce the messiah that the prophets had foretold. Perhaps they were expecting another burning bush like Moses had, but following an extra special star in the *sky* and an Angel in the *sky* who talked to shepherds seems to have been good enough. The people were crying for a deliverer, so they may have had to stretch things a bit to fit the prophecy. Most of the Jewish people didn't buy into the idea that Jesus was the Messiah, and still don't today. That is why Judaism is not Christianity.

Judaism teaches that God came to Moses on a mountain in a fiery chariot. In the form of a burning bush he gave him rules to live by, carved into two stone tablets. (Burning bush, fiery chariot, unidentified flying objects in the *sky*; I wonder?) These are the Ten Commandments that we have in the Old Testament. This God was adamant that he didn't want the Israelites to worship any other Gods before him. Who might they have been? It is reported that they were the Egyptian Gods. Where did all these "Gods" come from? OH MY GOD!!

The word Christ is actually a VERB. To be Christed, is to have the consciousness that goes beyond physical matter, and to have power and dominion over it... I believe from my studies of what Jesus was able to accomplish, he was indeed a Christ, an avatar, a Saint and a master teacher. It is highly possible that Jesus did bring the Logos (truths) back to Earth, in spite of all the propaganda that surrounded his life. It appears that every 2 to 3 thousand years an advanced master soul volunteers to bring the higher truths to us again. Perhaps, it takes about that long for the Logos to get as convoluted as they are today. I do not think that Jesus was the ONLY son of God, and became a God in a physical body. The royal blood of Jesus could mean that the blood of the Skygods was more prevalent in his genes. That may be why he was a very advanced being, and displayed such extraordinary talents. His message has been interpreted and added to so many times that very little of it remains intact. It might be just about time for another great master to restate the core "truths". I believe it is more important to receive his message than argue about his origin.

Jesus reportedly said that we can do the things he did and even more. He is telling us who we are and how we can change our life. He said, "I and the Father are <u>One</u>". If you don't take that to mean he is God, but saying he is a part of God or made of God, things take on a different tone. Once you understand the oneness of everything, the actual teachings of Jesus make much better sense. His message was sound, but what they have done with it is tragic.

There is a book out called *"The Five Gospels". In it, linguists got together and tried to figure out scientifically what Jesus really said and what was added to it in later interpretations. It is difficult to understand what someone means when you listen to them in everyday language. Did you play the telephone game when you were kids? Do you remember how different the final message was from the one first told? It is virtually impossible to really get the true meaning of something said 2000 years ago. The linguists found that about 10 percent of the New Testament was likely spoken in the time of, or by Jesus. We have a huge lack of validated information about what he really said and did.

There have been as many translations of what he taught as there are people with agendas that his teachings need to fulfill. There was also a strong political agenda around him which is still prevalent today. I believe Jesus to have been an enlightened master, but it isn't important one way or the other what you believe about this. Jesus acquired the "Christ consciousness", just as Siddhartha acquired the "Buddha Nature". The words Christ and Buddha are descriptive terms telling of an advanced Spiritual being. In other words they, *"Got IT "and of course with "Getting IT" comes the desire to share "IT".*

CHAPTER 19

Eastern Religion

I had the privilege of taking Refuge in the Dharma in Woodstock NY at the Karma Kagyu Monastery, while visiting my husband. These are my understandings about the nature of Buddhism. Their basic tenant is Mindfulness and Compassion for all sentient beings. By mindfulness, they mean keeping your monkey mind in check. The major realization of Siddhartha when he became the Buddha was that the middle way was the only way to achieve enlightenment. The Buddhists teach the middle way of being *in this world, but not of it*. All excessive behavior is destructive. You can have too much or too little of anything, and cause imbalance in your life. Rising above the trap of duality is their goal. Essentially, they are teaching how to get out of the time trap.

Hinduism is one of the oldest religions on the planet, dating back thousands of years. Hinduism is to Buddhism what Judaism is to Christianity. Eastern philosophy believes that the soul reincarnates again and again, to earn enough "merit" to get off the wheel of birth and death. They call the physical side of life Maya or Samsara, which are confusion, illusion and suffering. To the extent that we have to forget everything we know about our larger existence, so that we can play the game of life without 'cheating', it truly seems like suffering. In the Eastern view, suffering is always yearning for the otherness of things. It is being attached to the physical world and allowing it to define you, instead of being in your Buddha or Brahma nature which is all inclusive and needs nothing.

Buddhists are not teaching about any first cause or creator of the universe. They are teaching about how to realize the oneness of all beings. It is in the acceptance of *what is* that one finds Nirvana. Nirvana is likened to heaven, and is a peaceful compatibility with "All that IS". It is a state of mind, not a place to go. Buddha teaches that it is only when we cease to resist the situations of life and rise above them, that suffering ends and enlightenment begins. This sounds very nice, but few can really "get this" and very few achieve it. The material world has a very strong pull, and our personal story gets in the way of our happiness. The Eastern picture of life and Spirit make our little personal circumstances just passing happenings that hold no power to upset us.

Eastern philosophy teaches that everything we do is creating karma that either enhances, or deters us. Compassion is a large part of Eastern teaching, because they know that we are all stuck on the wheel of birth and death. Compassion is not feeling sorry for someone. Being compassionate is acknowledging that we are all born into an imperfect human body, and we will all make mistakes on our way to enlightenment. Buddhism teaches acceptance and compassion for all beings that are still on the wheel of suffering.

Stepping on the path toward enlightenment is becoming aware that what happens in life, to us and to others, is all a process toward breaking the cycle of rebirth. Not having to reincarnate is a form of graduation. Before enlightenment, the idea of coming back here is desirable. We cling to our human bodies and our human existence, because that is what we identify as our *"self"*. We don't want to lose self, and if we have to die, we want to get back in the game as quickly as possible. After enlightenment not coming back here is a worthy goal. To get off the crazy wheel of birth and death, and be in your Buddha Nature, is liberation.

Siddhartha acquired his Buddha Nature while sitting under a Bodhi tree in meditation. From time to time a human being acquires the full Buddha Nature and refreshes the teachings for those who follow Buddhism. A Bodhisattva is what they call a soul that volunteers to come back in to the physical world after enlightenment, in order to help others find their way out. An approximate equivalent in Christianity might be John the Baptist.

Buddhists and Hindus believe that we are returned to physical life based on the merit we collected in the last life. This merit, or lack of it, is called karma. It will be your karma to have a fortunate or unfortunate rebirth, arrived at by your past choices in other lifetimes. They teach that you do not have any say in your choice of births. It is all based on past actions, period!

Meditation is a large part of Eastern Religious practices. Meditation is a way to touch the Spirit that you are... Many of you think of meditation as doing nothing but sitting and contemplating your navel. You don't realize until after you experience it, that a different world opens up once your monkey mind is quiet, and you are at peace with your surroundings, and circumstances.

A monk in a monastery in Tibet can have riches beyond measure, because he has learned acceptance and compassion. While sitting under a tree watching the flowers grow, he is rich in Spirit. That same monk could focus on the fact that his country is now China, and that bad things happen in the world, and he becomes poor in Spirit. This is not wishful thinking or avoidance of the world. It is a calm knowledge that both sides of duality exists. It is his choice to think as he will. His teachings have shown him that the way to happiness, amid the world of Maya, is to accept the world as it is and watch it with compassion. He meditates with the intent to hold the world in his mind as perfect. This can also be said of any other discipline that shows the way to peacefulness, and acceptance of all beings on their path toward enlightenment.

Some advanced Hindu and Buddhist monks are in meditation almost all the time. They have mastered the physical body and transcended it. Many masters have performed seemingly miraculous feats. Jesus walked on water, Buddha made flowers grow, and Yogis can control their body temperature to melt show and levitate. Many miracles have been reported by countless witnesses in modern times. These are not just old stories that happened thousands of years ago. I have heard that even now, an advanced yogi must master the art of walking on water as part of his advancement.

I personally have witnessed a Rinpoche' (the equivalent of a Catholic Bishop or high priest) turn into his rainbow body and become translucent. I have seen a man part the waters with his mind, at the Potomac River. I suppose I too could walk on water if I really studied and put the energy into it, but I am way too lazy. I am not a Buddha or a Jesus, or a Brahma, but I am made from the same stuff. I don't have a Guru in this lifetime, but I am pretty sure that I have had many in my past lives. I enjoy following Mooji on YouTube and if I were to choose a Guru he would be the one. I feel a deep connection to India and Tibet. My lesson in this lifetime is to witness and experience more than one path. I have already had my share of mountain top lifetimes. I also have past life recall of being a Nun, and I am having *none* of that in this lifetime!

CHAPTER 20

Pagan & Nature Religions

The word Pagan basically means, not Christian. It was actually thrown out by the Catholic Church as a slur. The early Christian church went on Witch hunts to stomp out anyone that followed the "old ways", which was just about everyone until they were *persuaded* to conform. Pagans worship the Earth Goddess and consider her to be sacred. They believe the Earth is sacred, and that she is a living being.

I was able to view the planet Saturn through a high powered telescope. I was awestruck by the awareness that the planet that I was looking at was alive. Just as you can tell if an animal is just sleeping or dead, you can see the life force of the planets. It would be a safe assumption that Gaia also is a living being. When you wrap your head around the idea that you are living on a living being, it becomes sacred. Mother Nature really is alive and has intent. The quip, It's not nice to upset Mother Nature, becomes much more relevant. OOPS!... I think we are being bad children. If we don't grow up enough to keep our Gaia clean and healthy, Momma is going to be mad. I think it might be too late. I think Mom is mad!!

I saw a bumper sticker that sums up Nature Religion perfectly, "Tree Hugging Dirt Worshiper". How can that be so bad? It certainly isn't someone to be feared, unless you are not secure in your own beliefs. Goddess worshipers do not negate the oneness of all beings. They are including the one great being we live on.

Intolerance of other belief systems happens with all religions and Pagan religions are just as guilty as the rest. If you are not threatened by a belief system that does not believe exactly like yours, you might be an older soul. This is a young soul planet, but not all souls here are young. Hopefully, there are enough elders here to keep the young ones from doing irreparable damage.

I know that there are many people who want to be big bad scary witches. Many people, who feel powerless in their life, want to make a show of power, especially supernatural power. What they don't know, is that the power they seek does not come from wearing particular clothing, or making a show of any belief system. Real power comes from deep within the heart. A serious Wiccan, who has studied the religion in depth, comes to learn that there is only one power, and that power needs to be used for good. They understand the law of attraction, and that what you put out comes back to you. This is especially true if you practice magic to create circumstances. A definition of the word Magic is, "the ability to change the state of consciousness at will". Consciousness is what attracts circumstances. Pagan religions are noted for ritual practices such as potions and amulets. It does not matter if you are burning sage, chasing the eye of Newt or spreading salt, because it is the physical actions that anchor your intentions.

> The Wiccan code is very simple and beautiful. This is the short version.
>
> *Abide the Wiccan Rede ye must*
> *In Perfect love and perfect trust*
> *Eight words the Wiccan rede fulfill*
> *As ye harm none, do as ye will*
> *Ever mind, the power of three*
> *What ye send out, comes back to thee*
> *Follow this with mind and heart*
> *Merry Meet and Merry Part.*

Native American cultures worship The Sky God and Mother Earth. They respect all animal, vegetable, and mineral life, and see every aspect of life as sacred. They preform rituals around the seasons of the year just as the Wiccan and other Shamanic traditions do. All nature religions follow the wheel of the year, and are focused on the Earth, and her continuing bounty. Nature religions study natural medicines. They are excellent botanists, and want all things organic.

The potions and love spells that are popular (as fodder for television) are a small part of the picture. A spell will work because of the belief in it. By engaging both the physical and mental aspects of your desire, you can attract your goals much more easily. A "spell" to bring a relationship into your life, is better anchored in consciousness, with something tangible like a rose, than just imagining your goal. The medicine bag of the Shaman holds symbols of power and desire. When you cast a circle, or a medicine wheel you are creating a space "between" the manifested and un-manifested reality. Your circle is sacred space from which you can declare your desire, and impregnate it with your intent. To watch a Voodoo queen whipping herself into an altered state, to make something happen might look bizarre to an American from Iowa. Watching an evangelist whip up the crowd with "can we have an AMEN" is the same thing, just sounding different. There are as many seemingly strange ritual practices, as there are people of the world that think them up. All religions create sacred space, be it a circle, medicine wheel, temple, mosque or cathedral.

CHAPTER 21

The Page-ites

I n my ministry, I use a story I call "The Page-ites" as an example of how our religions have gone off the mark. I use a man I call James for this illustration.

James was standing on a mountain top one day praying to God for answers. He wanted to know the "right" way to conduct his affairs. He was afraid that he would make a mistake and that God would *get him* if he did something wrong. God heard his prayer and saw his sincerity. Behold the sky opened up and the voice of God spoke to him... "James, I have the answers you seek". Beautiful golden pages began to fall from the clouds and land at James's feet. The most profound wisdom was written on the pages. God told James that if he read them, he would have the answers he desired. Then he was to destroy them by pounding them to dust. God said, "It will be by your word and example that others will come to know how to live a joyous life, in the Grace of God". Then the sky darkened and God left James to do as he was told.

After James read the pages, he went home with his precious pages and read them over and over feverishly. He invited his friends and neighbors in to see the pages. They began to change their lives in accord with the writing on the pages. Then along came others who did not agree with what the pages said. More people came who did not even read the pages, but were afraid they said something that would offend their brand of God. They conspired to destroy the pages, because they did not agree with what their Gods taught. Others thought that they didn't mean things the same way and reinterpreted them to make them "*clearer*".

James's people banded together in an effort to keep the pages safe and pure. They put them inside a stone structure and only the original friends and neighbors were allowed near them. They felt that they had to form an armed guard to protect the pages. Now the others were doubly outraged and set up an army of their own to stamp out the pages. War ensued; famine and killing spread throughout the land. As things got bleaker and bleaker, James went back up to the mountain and began to flail his fists in the air. He called on the voice of God to tell him what to do about the horrors they faced, while protecting the pages. The sky again opened up and again the voice of God spoke and said... "My dear James, this was between you and me. I told you to read the word, not protect the pages"...

How very much like a child James is in this story. He wants to do well, but can't without rules. Then of course he breaks the rules and tries to do things his way. Later after creating chaos, he goes back to his parent and says, "What did I do wrong to deserve this"? When the James' of this world grow up, we will not have to create wars to protect what we can learn by listening to the word of God within our own heart and mind. If we were truly meant to all read the same pages, there would be pages aplenty, falling from the sky at all times.(*I'm sure God would not run out of ink).*

I feel that the story of James is a good rendition of what has happened to the world's religions They are all shouting from their pulpits that we are going to war over their version of the pages. No matter which religion we subscribe to, it is apparent that we are created by something and it follows, that we are here for some purpose. It also follows, that our purpose will sooner or later be accomplished. It might be better to apply logic to what you believe, instead of running on autopilot. Ask for the pages yourself and then pound them into dust and live in Joy and Thanksgiving.

The Mess We Are Making
And How To Fix It

Chapter 22

Addictions

O n this young soul planet, at this time, the rise of addiction is off the charts. It appears that more and more people are choosing to escape life by using some form of addictive behavior. It's as if they are covering their heads and trying to run away from the fear of living life in their present environment. The addiction menu is huge... It doesn't have to be a substance. You can get hooked on the rush of video gaming, gambling, or sex; anything that takes you out of yourself and makes you feel bigger and grander than you see yourself to be. There are many people who just want to zone out and not know what is going on. Alcohol is so last year, now we have designer drugs. I don't mean to slight alcohol because it is stronger than ever. Leave it to this generation of exceptionally material people, to create "designer" poison. There is no ending to bigger and better, even if it kills you. Children are taught at an early age, that everything is dangerous and must be feared. Fear feeds any form of addictive behavior. The young souls want to cover their heads, because there are monsters under the bed

Our medical community works under the assumption that the body is who we are, and it is a machine. You get the message that if you are not happy, just take this pill. There are millions of people who are on prescribed "feel good" drugs, and are viewing the world through a windshield. By ramping up the "feel good" chemicals in your brain, you avoid the feelings associated with living in our society. Unfortunately, if you don't look at a problem, you can't fix it. There is a difference between choosing to avoid negativity and hiding from it. Keeping yourself away from people and situations that are toxic to your life is definitely a good thing. Using anything that masks the situation is not a benefit to your life. Addictive behavior is a response to fear of events, or feelings that deeply hurt you. The fear of being emotionally hurt is often stronger than the fear of being physically hurt.

While I was studying to be an addiction counselor, I was overwhelmed with the awareness that everywhere I looked; I saw the effects of addiction. From my vantage point at the time it was primarily alcohol that had been passed down from generation to generation. I couldn't find anyone who was not touched, in some way, by an influential relative who was alcoholic. When you grow up around an addict or alcoholic you are scarred by the, *"crazy making"*, that the addiction creates. I was very depressed by what looked like something we couldn't avoid or overcome.

I did what I always do when I need to find answers; I went to my inner Spiritual wisdom and asked for help. I prayed about it and what I heard in my higher mind was, "Addiction is a lesson that every soul must experience on its journey toward enlightenment". The only way out of addiction is by surrendering to your Spiritual essence. I was also told that it is always a *'crap shoot lifetime'*, because overcoming addiction often takes more than one lifetime. On the plus side overcoming addiction guarantees a *"Spiritual leap"*. I would say "I'll pass", but I am sure I have experienced my lifetimes of addiction and now I am choosing to help others find their way out of theirs.

We are taught that someone has to *"hit bottom"* before they can conquer addiction. I suspect that your Higher Self keeps trying to get your attention and finally, when all is lost, it creates a major crisis in the hope that you might notice that something needs to change in your life. The only way I can be effective as an addictions counselor is to realize that it is OK to die drunk and give it another go, in another lifetime. I know that sounds cold, but I assure you it is not. To me, when I watched good people kill themselves slowly, that is the only way I am able to cope. I have to keep in mind that souls are eternal but bodies are not.

Before I begin the next section, I feel the need to state first and foremost that all Medical professionals are not crooks. There are many fine, compassionate people who try to help others. I have heard some of them complain that they cannot practice medicine, because the insurance companies will not let them do what they need to do for their patients.

In our times, it is not as easy to identify addictive behavior, because of the lovely pharmaceuticals that are prescribed. Mom can be zoned out daily and it is supposed to be OK, because the *"Doctor said* "she was sick. If you are truly in pain and there is no possible end in sight, being zoned out is humane. I am speaking about <u>unnecessary</u> prescription drug abuse. . If you're sick, you can't be blamed for being stoned. That is the disguise used with an addiction to prescription drugs. The addiction takes on a life of its own and it will cause you to stay sick to feed it's self. Once the addiction is out of control, one of two things will be the outcome. You die from an overdose that they might call something else, because of medical malpractice, OR, you are buying more pills on the street, because your doctor has noticed that you are abusing the prescriptions and stops prescribing them to you. You can either get caught and end up in jail, die, or become financially bankrupt and homeless.

To say that addiction might be a life choice is hard to swallow, but once you begin to own your soul choices and karmic conditions, the feeling of total victimhood dissolves and it is easier to find your inner strength. Some of the pitiful addicts in the homeless shelters might be volunteering, on a soul level, to bring the problem of addiction into stark reality for those who view their misery. They might also be offering an opportunity for others to demonstrate compassion. We cannot assume that all homeless addicts are poor young souls who have lost their way. Each person's life path is suited to their own unique purpose, and that my friends, is why it isn't good to judge others." Judge not lest ye be judged" takes on a whole new meaning when we look at addiction or any other life choice in relationship to soul growth.

If you view addiction in your life as a lesson, you naturally look for a way to learn from it. If you view any condition or event as a potential threat, you will focus on the harm and attract more of it. If you look at life as a journey of your own choosing, you will rise slightly above the suffering, and see that the journey can be valuable, if you choose it to be. All addiction is avoidance of something therefore; all addiction is due to fear. You can't see the reason for the addiction, while you are lost in the physical conditions of it. The addiction seems to take on a life of its own and clouds your vision to see its destructive nature. Meditation allows you to step out of *"the story of you"*. From a vantage point that seems to be outside you, it is possible to reach back into yourself, and begin to heal yourself. Addictions are so common now that it is amazing when a person is *not* addicted to something.

In my own life, I was deprived of a father due to alcohol, and was left with a mother who was emotionally damaged by her co-dependent relationship with him. My father committed suicide when he learned he had cirrhosis of the liver and could no longer drink. I did not know him well, and thankfully was not close to him, but he deeply affected my life by his absence. His Father and Uncle were alcoholic and died within days of each other from drinking bad moonshine. Addiction weaves a tight web around most of our lives, in one way or another. If you don't see it in your life, I would say you are very fortunate. I would also bet that if you ask the right questions, you will likely find out differently..

Rev. Lorana Clark

Desperate old men

Spirit gave me a vivid dream that let me know how addiction affected my grandparents, and perhaps great grandparents. In the dream, I was witnessing a scene around a potbelly stove in a general store. There were many men sitting around the stove in deep despair. I could feel their acute depression, and feelings of inadequacy. There was no work, and they could not provide for their families. They were passing around a jug, and getting drunk to avoid the feelings of being failures as men. The feeling was heart and gut wrenching. A small boy dressed in knickers came into the store. He had been at the dry goods store, asking for a job sweeping the stoop. He was perhaps 4 or 5 years old and trying to be a man himself. When the shop keeper asked him how much he wanted to be paid, he said a dime, instead of the penny he had been instructed to ask for. He did not understand the denominations of money. The shop keeper kicked at him, and sent him out with slurs of insults and profanity, for expecting such a high wage. He went back to the store to report what had happened to his father, who then beat him in a drunken rage, for being so stupid. I woke from that dream knowing that those were my father's relatives, and perhaps the small boy had been my father, or my grandfather. It took a day or two to shake that forlorn feeling. I will never forget how those men felt. I also knew why they turned to alcohol to avoid that deep pain.

CHAPTER 23

The Media

The media informs society of what it takes to be 'cool', and aids addiction in a variety of ways. Celebrities are falling to the poison of addiction and letting the whole world watch as they are being filmed in recovery. The media has a hand in what drives people to addictive behavior, and also brings it out into the open and shows the world that anyone can fall prey to its seduction.

Our young teens want to be "cool" and fit in. Why do they feel the pressing need to fit in? Is it all genetics? Why do *30somethings* feel the pressure of needing to fit in, or to have more stuff? Why does the gang member feel the need to fit in?? Nobody seems to feel good enough. Everyone wants to identify or, "belong" to something. The pack mentality of the instinctual being that we inhabit seems to need to be fulfilled. On that same note, being alone or ostracized is akin to death in the instinctual mind. Who will be the alpha, and who is always supposed to be omega? Low self-esteem is a common denominator in all of this, which creates fertile ground for addictions to manifest. How can we have good self-esteem when we set ourselves apart, judge ourselves harshly, and have no pack to compare ourselves to?

The media promotes the ideas we have about what it means to fit in. The conflicting message we receive is that we need to fit in, but it is good to be different. We are also told that we need to set ourselves apart, and it is dangerous to let people get too close to us. It depends on what the media wants to sell. One of the answers appears to be creating an alternate self on the internet. We can create a virtual community and not have to leave the house. We create puppets of ourselves and make them dance. I have met people who live most of their lives in virtual reality on the internet.

Our society is largely based on fear, because the economy is based on our need for supply. We are inundated with messages of lack and fear from every possible media, in order to sell us safety and success. If we are afraid of the sun, we will need to buy sunscreen, and then of course vitamin D, because we stay out of the sun. We are told to keep our children safe and buy helmets. We are shamed or fined if we don't follow what the media decides is safe. Lobbyists make seat belt laws then car companies and insurance companies all benefit from our feeling afraid. I am not advocating putting others in danger. I am saying however, that there is big money in selling fear. There is always a commercial to get more, do better, go faster, have the most sex, money or whatever experience which brings with it a feeling of euphoria or superiority. These ideas set up perfect breeding ground for all forms of addiction. I could go on with an entire book on these advertising contradictions, but the bottom line is; our world promotes fear to sell safety.

The media does not limit itself to enhancing addictive behavior. The media also promotes the most popular disease, and promotes the fear that helps create the illness in the minds and of the masses. This in turn, feeds the medical machine. By promoting fear, they create what to be afraid of. This is the <u>literal</u> truth. What we put in the collective mind enough times becomes the truth, or the habit. Once you have accepted an idea, it takes root in your consciousness. By fearing a disease you attract that disease to you, and *Big Pharm* has just the pill to cure it. The side effects might kill you, but there is another pill for that too!

Insurance companies thrive on fear of loss. If you have enough insurance when something bad happens, you are covered. Because of the law of attraction, selling insurance attracts loss. Insurance companies are in so much financial trouble that they can no longer pay for what they are selling. *Gee; I wonder why?* Remember that what you put your attention on is what you feed. If you are afraid of loss, loss happens. If you promote a fear of loss, to sell protection, you will attract loss not protection. When someone builds a wall, they expect an adversary, and will attract a set of circumstances that will tear it down. If they build a fortress, they will attract someone to invade it. If they build trust, they attract trustworthiness. If you know within yourself that you are safe, you are protected

In this media driven society, our desires can drive us to success, or drive us crazy. We can become so obsessed with success that we end up depressed. We run from the fear of failure and inadequacy. No matter how hard we try we can't overcome the deep feeling that something is lacking. We either run from that feeling of lack, or try to cover it up with drugs, drink, food, sex, or some other form of addictive behavior.

The clergy will tell you it is God you are lacking, and that you need to be saved from your sinful self. Entire organizations are kept alive by fear, while selling hope, and a loving forgiving father for the young souls to lean on. Even in the best of times, someone is always there with a warning. We end up believing that something bad is always just around the corner. It is almost as if when something good happens, it will have to be paid for with something bad coming later. Our culture is based on something going wrong, so someone can get paid to fix it.

Happiness is portrayed by a carnival atmosphere, where there are thrills and chills all the time but, will ultimately have to end. We seem to believe that happiness has a price tag that very few have the currency to pay for. Contentment does not sell goods and services. As far as the media and the economy are concerned, *it's not OK to be happy with life as it is*. We are programmed to seek progress, for progress' sake. We have to make work, so that the giant population has something to do and something to buy.

CHAPTER 24

Surrender

S urrender is a huge step toward overcoming any addictive behavior. At some point in the journey toward healing we learn about the need to surrender. That certainly goes against the grain. It seems counterproductive to our striving. Surrender we say, OH NO... I am a survivor. I have to fight this monkey on my back. If I surrender I lose! I have to be in control of my life! These two concepts, control and surrender don't seem to be compatible. Being a survivor can become an ego-based ideal. The rub is that when we identify proudly as a survivor; we attract all sorts of things into our lives that we have to survive, so that we can feel proud of ourselves. Surrender sounds like giving up, and certainly not surviving. Given time, we come to understand that surrender is the next step to success. By surrender, I don't mean that you should give all your belongings to charity and walk with an alms bowl. If you have chosen a completely Spiritual and minimal life path, and you are walking with an alms bowl, you are likely not reading this book.

There is a difference between surrender and resignation. You might be homeless and standing in line at the soup kitchen, feeling hopeless and having given up. You are *resigned* to your lot in life and no longer put any effort into improving your situation. Surrender is crying *Uncle*; then getting up and taking a different approach to your problem. Surrender doesn't mean you just let someone abuse you; it is about accepting the fact that you are being abused, or are in an undesirable situation that you can't find your way out of. Once you surrender you are free to use your energy to change your situation instead of using it to resist *what is*. Doing the same thing over and over and expecting different results is the definition of Crazy. In truth, trying to fix your problems without surrendering to them first is acting crazy.

Once striving for self-importance in the material world subsides, surrender to *'what is'* becomes very fulfilling. You will not feel the pressure to fit in, or not fit in as the case may be. It becomes less important to have the nicest most luxurious vehicle or home. You will just want to get yourself from one place to another easily and live comfortably, with the least amount of hassle and maintenance. You might decide to ride the bus or live in a smaller abode. When you surrender, what is in your outer circumstances no longer defines you. This is the surrender of the material world, with its judgments and measurements of your success. It is the loosening grip of the damaged ego-self. The ego-self is the part of you that is married to the belief that you have to have a certain outer identity in order to be good enough or bad enough to be accepted. When you cry *Uncle*, you give up on trying to cover up or run away from your fears and perceived inadequacies. The reason for the addictive behavior can then be brought to light and healed.

Many people think the ego is all bad, but in fact, it is not. We need a healthy ego to be able to set good boundaries and choose happiness. In the land of duality, you can't choose oneness unless you know separateness. The ego is necessary to be an individual in this life. We need to be individuals to experience the learning and growth that we have set up for ourselves. On the grand scale we are all one in Spirit. While in the game of life, we have to have individuality to be able to play.

Pain Body

We bring the ego-self into each life, with the karma we are trying to heal. It is the part of our soul that is learning and growing. It is the part that doesn't know that it is all part of God-stuff. It is called the egoic mind and it lives in the subconscious, and runs on autopilot. In his book *"A New Earth" Eckhart Tolle' calls a damaged egoic mind, a pain body. You have a physical body, and emotional body, a mental body, and now a pain body.

The last thing the damaged ego- pain body wants to do is surrender. It believes that it needs power in the physical world to survive. Ironically it does, because if you take away its power to attract pain, you take away its existence. *(Re-*

read the last two sentences, because it is very important that you understand this) You can certainly live without it, but it cannot live without your belief in suffering. If you totally identify with your physical reality, survival is difficult and happiness is dependent on how you can defend what you have. Addiction makes you feel good and powerful, even though it ends up making you feel bad and powerless, which is what the underlying pain body believes is right to start with. The pain body will fight to keep the brokenness in place. When two people on autopilot get together, the pain bodies are free to dance their destructive dances. They will feed off each other by acting out and inflict all forms of suffering on themselves and each other. The law of attraction is working perfectly, showing you what your inner belief about yourself is, through the other person.

Since we set up our life lessons and quite often the major players in our personal drama, it would follow that individuals with matching pain bodies would attract each other. If you have been dancing with this same partner for more than one lifetime, you will try again to heal the problems between you. Your pain bodies are carried from one lifetime into the next, by the laws of karma. If your pain body needs to be beaten to feel normal, you will certainly attract someone whose pain body needs to accommodate you. If you need to be a victim, you will attract a perpetrator. You might think that if you are a kind and loving doormat, you will attract someone who appreciates your sacrifice. It does not work that way! A doormat's purpose is to be stepped on. It all comes down to the health of your ego, and the awareness of who you really are...which is a Spiritual being having a human experience.

Generosity is a beautiful thing and when it is done with a genuine desire to serve others it is beautiful, but many people want to be seen as generous for the wrong reasons. What do some donors get out of donating? They get a *feeling of goodness*. They need to give and be recognized as a giver, to feel good about themselves. The gift is then an ego gift that has lots of strings attached. Those strings will surely be left hanging, by whomever they bestow their gifts upon. The pain body is doing the giving and needs to feel the pain of rejection and lack of appreciation. This is what I believe the great teacher Jesus was speaking of when he said in Mathew 6:2, *"So when you give to the needy, do not announce it with trumpets, as the hypocrites do in the synagogues and on the streets, to be honored by others. Truly I tell you, they have received their reward in full.* [3] *But when you give to the needy, do not let your left hand know what your right hand is doing,* [4] *so that your giving may be in secret. Then your Father, who sees what is done in secret, will reward you"*. If the inner climate of the individual is truly goodness, they will not need outer recognition for their gifts. If we are self-aware of whom we really are, which is a part of God, then not only does sharing, giving, and receiving make sense, they the natural things to do. If the pain body is in charge, the giver never feels *appreciated* and the receiver feels *"beholden"*.

Good self-esteem is not a "big ego", it is a healthy ego. A big ego needs to prove its worth to the outer world, so that the world can validate what the person doesn't truly believe on the inside. This is really low self-esteem. A self-aware person has nothing to prove to the outer world and lives in a simple state of joy. You don't need to stop participating in the everyday world but if difficulties arise they are assessed and dealt with from an acceptance of *what IS.*

The Serenity Prayer is all about surrender. It states; "Grant me the serenity to accept the things I cannot change. Change the things I can, and (most importantly) the wisdom to know the difference. Once someone has accepted their dependence on a substance or behavior they can put a bit of distance between their inner spirit and the problem. It is their job to then keep themselves away from the circumstances that trigger the pain body to act out. It is an art to be able to know when to fight and when to run from people, places, and situations. Meditation and other techniques that help you stay in touch with your inner GodSelf are priceless when overcoming addictions. We are then embracing the God inside of each of us.

In summary: to surrender, we need to really understand the concept of nonresistance. Not resisting is accepting what is as, What IS. Non-resistance is not passively accepting everything; it is consciously choosing to let some things pass, by giving them no place to rest inside you. I believe one of the reasons the old AA and NA programs are successful is that they employ, first off, the concept of nonresistance. The statement "hello my name is _____, and I am an alcoholic or addict or both" is one of acceptance of What Is. Where I believe that AA and NA can go off the mark is when the "I AM" statement continues to decree the truth about yourself long after the need to face "what IS" has been met. Let these statements define your current condition while you are discovering it. Later in the program it might be better to say, "Hello my name is _____ and I am a recovering alcoholic. Claiming your success, once you have truly achieved it, will help you maintain it.

I use this story to make the idea of surrender and acceptance more understandable to the folks that I work with.

Mud Bog

I have Boys and they have trucks.

Down by the river flat on a cold autumn day, the "boys" take their trucks out to see who can get through the big mud pit that has been created over the summer by the rise and fall of the water. This is some form of annual male bonding ritual that I do not totally understand (snicker). The trucks go in, and of course one gets stuck... The driver rocks it back and forth, spinning the tires trying desperately to free the truck. His knuckles are white while gripping the steering wheel, as he tries and tries to get out of the pit. His frustration mounts as his truck gets stuck deeper and deeper. This is known as resistance to What IS.

Finally the truck is so deep in the mud that he can't even open the door to get out. With resignation, the driver crawls out the window, and has to climb onto the hood to be able to jump to firm ground. This is surrender, and a leap of faith, because no one is really sure if he can jump that far, especially in his "condition". All this becomes acceptance of What IS.

Now comes the real teaching ...Once he is on solid ground, he whips out his cell and calls his buddy to come with a chain to pull him out of the mud. After acceptance and surrender, corrective action can be taken. Rocking back and forth in frustration, using all the will power he has, gets him stuck deeper and deeper in his own mud. It is also a good idea to ask for help, and surrender to the idea that you are not going to be able to do it alone.

There is an alternative outcome to this story. One of the boys, (thankfully not my son) just kept fighting what IS, until there was no pulling him out. Resistance is futile! He had to leave his truck overnight. It rained and froze that night and did not thaw again until spring. His truck stayed all winter in the frozen mud. This was his only vehicle and his wife divorced him. You might think she was terribly intolerant, but this was not his first fight with the mud he was making of his life. This goes to show what can happen if you stubbornly cling to doing the same thing over and over expecting different results. (In the spring they cut the truck up and scrapped it.)

We have to stop, assess the situation from a different perspective, and then we are clear headed enough to make a new plan for success. In a world where we all really understood that we are all one family, asking for help would not be such a difficult thing to do either. When you wake up to whom you really are, you will accept your life journey and finally feel complete within yourself.

Chapter 25

Meditation

Meditation helps you step outside of your "story" and overcome addiction. Being able to step outside of your story and connect with your SoulSelf, for even a short period of time, will allow you to observe your story, instead of being immersed in it. The addiction can be placed one step back, and you can see that it has your physical life. In meditation you realize that nothing can touch the real you, which is your SoulSelf. The SoulSelf can help you step away from the addictive behavior. Your SoulSelf and your Higher Power, which is a term used in support groups, is referring to the same thing. The physical being cannot overcome addictions alone because its physiology has become dependent on the substance it is addicted to. It is your SoulSelf that will bolster you and give you freedom from addictions. In the present moment of meditation, however brief, you get in touch with your *real power*, not your *will power*. Once you get past the initial withdrawal phase , you can see the big picture from the vantage point of SoulSelf, and outer circumstances lose some of their importance. Life becomes much more peaceful and fulfilling. You will have an awareness of life as a Spiritual experience, and that is liberating.

Meditation is a powerful tool for growth, healing and awareness on all levels, not just when working with addictions. I can hear you now... "Oh yes meditation would be NICE, but I don't have time". You are right, you don't have time. Time isn't real, except for here in the physical. If you choose to, you can make time to meditate. Remember that ritual trains the physical. If you make yourself sit down for 5 minutes in the morning and 5 minutes before bed, you will create a habit. I guarantee you it is a better habit than smoking. I am literally saying to you that if you are smart you will make time for meditation. It will do more to insure your health and happiness than any pill or pleasure can come close to.

One of the worst things you can do is jump up and run in the morning when you first wake up. Wake up time is meant to be sacred. You are embracing your living dream and affirming yourself in it when you wake up. Create the discipline to get up easily, even if that means setting the dreaded alarm 10 minutes earlier. Set aside a few extra minutes to just be present in meditation. Much of our society does not honor anything but productivity, and it treats people like machines. You can choose otherwise. You can treat yourself to a bit of peace each morning and each evening, regardless of what the rest of your life is like. If you do this, the rest of your life will become less stressful and more joyful. I guarantee this to be true.

For most people quieting the monkey mind is next to impossible at first. If you tell your mind to be quiet it asks *why*. It is beneficial to simply pay attention to your breathing. Meditation is not problem solving or thinking, thinking, thinking. If your mind begins to chatter about what is happening in your life, you simply notice that, and then bring yourself back to paying attention to your breathing. Some people, when asked to quiet the mind feel threatened. Their mind is going in turbo charged motion all the time, and they like it that way. The pain body especially likes it that way. The last thing the pain body wants is for you to find a way to overcome your fears and worries. The negative self-talk is food for the pain body, and meditation has no room for self-talk of any kind.

If you are a person with a very fast mind, try using a mantra. A mantra is a phrase that you say over and over, which gives your mind something to do, while you are watching it do so. You will sooner or later get bored watching it work and drift into a peaceful state of *beingness,* instead of *doingness.* The goal is to get in touch with your essence, which is the very life force that you really are. It is the part of you that beats your heart. Even a few brief seconds of life force connection works magic in our lives.

Most people have a misconception about meditation from watching movies or television where monks are setting for hours, as if they were statues. I didn't know what to expect and thought it would be much harder than it is. I thought I would have to go through rigorous physical pain to meditate. There is no way I am going to sit for hours in one position and suffer through the pain that causes. In some schools of thought, you are taught to sit in a certain way and put your hands in a certain way. You are supposed to work through the discomfort, and focus your mind only on your inner self. If your mind wanders you can ask to be hit on the shoulder with a stick to bring your focus back into the moment. To me, that is a whole lot of something to do nothing. I know now that I can sip my coffee in the morning, and feel the presence of God in my heart. I know that it is good to discipline the mind and body. I prefer *not doing*. When we are not doing, we are *being*. When we put aside planning, thinking and remembering even for a brief moment, we have nothing left but self, true self, SoulSelf. I am sure there are many meditation instructors that will disagree with my coffee sipping meditation but, it works for me. I am a firm believer in "whatever works".

Meditation is like getting back to the baby's mind. When you look at a peaceful sleeping baby, and marvel at the beauty and grace the child appears to be in, you are looking at the quiet mind. A baby is still connected to the Spiritual realm. When you achieve a meditative state, you are back to where you were before you cluttered your mind with all the everyday junk that life has offered you. It is much easier to reconnect with your original life plan, when the monkey mind is quiet. You are in a state of Grace, and you are in touch with the Spiritual realm.

By sitting in a certain way or doing a certain thing we send a message to ourselves that something different is happening, and something important is going on. Engaging the body as well as the mind insures good results. I don't choose to be in pain while I meditate, and I don't stay in meditation for months on a mountain top. (I have had many mountain top lifetimes.) I am not a Spiritual Master in this lifetime but, I am a work in progress. My ritual is making the coffee and sitting comfortably by the window, basking in the sunlight or connecting with the stars.

Guided meditation is a wonderful tool that takes the work out of meditation. It is easy to just sit and listen to someone guiding your imagination on a healing journey. There are excellent guided meditations that will help you connect with your Higher Self and align your energies for optimal health and wellbeing. If you have balanced energy you have a natural tendency to meditate. If you are not balanced and meditate anyway, you will become balanced in your energy field. When all your energy is humming along smoothly, life becomes much less stressful and there is a natural tendency to seek Spirituality.

So many people feel empty in their lives and do not know what is missing. If they seek Spirituality from organized religion they are often left feeling guilty and shamed. If they get past that, they often end up feeling smug and arrogant, with a self- righteous attitude. They are then urged to convince their neighbors that they too need to join their exclusive club of truth. Meditation is a solitary pursuit. It requires no dogma of any kind. It is your right to sit quietly sipping tea, and watching the birds out the window.

There are many tapes you can listen to, or groups you can join, that will help you make a space for meditation. In a way this too is the pack mentality, but just as a gang can incite a riot, a group of meditators can incite peace. Christian literature states that God said "whenever two or more of you are together I am there". In meditation it doesn't take two for Spirit to be present. It takes the "I AM' presence of your SoulSelf. When you are present within your SoulSelf, everyone else is there by default, because you are tapped into the Oneness of "All that IS".

I must reiterate that meditation is not trying to do anything. It is a state *of Being, not Doing.* It doesn't really matter if you can sit in a lotus position for days, hours, or even minutes. It is helpful to have your back straight, if for no other reason than to let your chakra energy centers breathe, and function easily. A recliner might be nice, but you might simply fall asleep. Going from meditation to sleep is healthy for your body, but the sleep state is not the same as the gentle awareness of meditation. It is often helpful for me to listen to gentle music, and just let my mind ride on the notes.

Guided meditation is very beneficial, and can help you in so many ways. Even if you can't quiet your mind to meditate, you can listen to a soft discourse of inspirational words. If you have a desire to be more grounded, or loving, or for any goal you choose, you can either tape your own words, or purchase something someone else has recorded. If you are a beginner, I believe it is best to purchase meditation tapes. It is more important than you might think to have the right verbiage going into your subconscious, while in meditation.

I would suggest that you listen to audios that help you clean and balance your chakra energy. I am including a guided meditation in the back of this book that will help you ground your energy and cleanse your chakras. You can tape yourself reading it and play it back while you are sitting quietly. There are also many wonderful audio programs that will lift your life, and calm your Spirit available on the internet.

CHAPTER 26

Gray Matter

It is most helpful to realize that we are not our brains and that our brains are not all that thinks for us. Our brain is a collection of cells reacting to amino acids and hormones. The gray matter that we refer to as our brain is a focal point that has lots of nerves and chemicals in it. It takes what we experience with our <u>5 senses</u> and translates it to something we can perceive. It is also a mechanical instrument that is used for regulating the body functions. Chemical addictions alter the brain chemistry causing withdrawal symptoms when the chemical is taken away. This only lasts a short time. Seek medical help to allow your brain to right itself and then tend to the underlying cause of your need to alter your mind to begin with.

Consciousness is not just in your brain. There is consciousness in every cell of our body. One cell's consciousness is aware of all the other consciousness nearby and it interacts and reacts to them all the time. We are not our mind; we are the observer of our mind. We are life force energy. Our mind is like a closet for all that we perceive. We use brain to make sense of the 3d reality we live in. We are not our brain, and we are not our mind, but we use mind and brain as the conduit to bring our desires into physical form. We really have no way of knowing what any other mind perceives, because we can only know something from our own perspective. We really have no way of knowing if there is anyone else out there interacting with us. It could all be an illusion.

We use our brain muscle to process our senses and store data. Our brain is like a super computer. We have programs and subprograms and super programs, within our mind. Imagine your mind to be software, and your brain to be the hard drive on your personal computer. Your digestion, breathing, and all other automatic functions are devices that interact with the hard drive. We are basically a walking computer with feelings. *Oh goodie---"Data" has found emotion, and Pinocchio is a real boy.*

We have thought and memory in every cell and organ in our body. Our brain is not the only piece of hardware, and mind has millions of programs available. Transplant patients report having different ideas, likes, and dislikes after they have received someone else's cells. This has been labeled cellular memory.

Quantum physics states that everything is made of thought-things. We can never, at the quantum level, be separate from anything else. I call the measurements on the quantum level 'thought molecules'. Focused thought molecules pack a chair dense enough to sit in. We are projecting our thoughts all the time, creating and recreating our reality. It is our collective agreement that while here in 3D reality, walls are too hard to walk through, and chairs can be sat on.

You have a 3 part mind. Your *conscious* mind is what you use to decide to eat a sandwich, instead of a pizza. It is called deductive in its reasoning ability. Deductive means it can CHOOSE what is best, by the process of eliminating what it doesn't want. It has logic and reasoning capabilities (hopefully) and is the main participator in the illusion of duality. Your *subconscious* mind stores all the times you decided to eat a sandwich instead of a pizza, since the beginning of forever, and how eating the sandwich or pizza makes you *feel*. That part of your mind is called inductive. It has *no ability to choose*, it simply accepts what IS, with no logic involved. Your Spiritual or *super conscious* mind sends down the desire to eat in moderation from your Higher Self thereby preserving your health, and continuing your soul journey.

If you have negative feelings about eating that sandwich, a subprogram which is stored in the subconscious mind switches on and causes you to eat two sandwiches, or throw up the one you did eat. Everything depends on your underlying belief about food, and whether it's necessary to be fat or skinny. The particulars of your feelings only matter to you. If you feel good, you want to be joyful, and do fun and happy things. This adds to the pot of Joy... If you feel bad, you add depression to the pot of fear and you can't feel good, no matter what you are doing. The soul is learning to choose and learning that choices attract events.

The conscious mind at one time or another had to allow a negative subprogram to be created. If you were very young at the time it was created, you didn't have the choice to decide whether it was a good program or a bad one. The subprogram could even have come from another lifetime and carried over into this life. If it is a negative program, the pain body carried it in. It will need to be brought to light (enlightened) and healed. Mental health professionals drive Mercedes, thanks to the subconscious mind of their patients. You can dig around in the subconscious for years, ferreting out all the junk programs, or you can use your conscious mind to put in overriding programs. The existence of a harmful subprogram is obvious, if you are doing something destructive to yourself and you can't stop doing it.

Subprograms are not necessarily bad. You may be running a subprogram that says you enjoy healthy eating, and moderate exercise. A subprogram is a habit that is so entrenched in your subconscious, that you can't distinguish it from who you are. I used eating as an example, because it is so basic to existence, but it can be anything. Some popular areas for subprogram malfunction are: eating, drinking, drugging, gambling, sleeping, sexing, washing, sweating, shopping, to name a few. If you are OCD and have more ideas, feel free to add them here. It is the excesses that get us into trouble. You can have too much or too little of anything. I recommend the middle way, which is the Buddhist way of moderation. If you have a rogue subprogram sending signals to your desires, the middle way is next to impossible to maintain.

A rogue program might also be purposefully placed in your energy before you incarnated. If so, it is attached to a life lesson that is far more important than simply overcoming a pesky but destructive pattern like nail biting. The pain body is actually looking for healing, It just doesn't know it. You may identify with shyness or popularity, elitism or total self-depravation, being extra "good" or extra "bad". There is a wounded and a talented person in everyone. If there were nothing to work on, there would be no reason to come to Earth School in the first place. You would likely not be visiting this young soul planet, unless it is true that we fell into the time trap. In that case we still need to find our way out of it.

When you define yourself as Spirit, you rise above the physical mind and get in touch with the Spiritual mind. You move into the place where you are a witness to all that your body/mind is doing and thinking. You become a witness to the events in your life, instead of a puppet of them. When you can connect with yourself as the witness of your life, you are actually connecting with the super conscious Higher Power at the lowest rung of its Spiritual ladder. This is the place where you are in touch with your Higher Power.

You have a mind in your head and a mind in your heart. There is a gland very near your heart center called the thymus gland that translates <u>emotions</u> into chemical responses and affects the entire body. It is well known that emotions are important players in the health and wellbeing of the body. It is the thymus that processes love, joy, fear, anger and passion, and then informs the heart of the state that the emotional body is experiencing. It is very important to the health of your body, mind, and Spirit to keep your head and your heart minds connected, and bathed in love, not fear. The mind in your heart is much more powerful than the one in your head. The heart-mind is connected to the Spiritual essence of all of life. Perhaps, it could be called the Soul mind. It is certainly the mind where your witness lives. We are learning that energetically hooking up the brain with the heart creates wonderful results. When you bridge the 18 inch gap between your heart and your brain you are connected to everything in a unifying way.

The Heart Mind creates a grid of energy. Imagine that there is an electrical grid around you emanating from your heart and expanding out around the globe. It is connecting your heart to every other heart. Just like an electrical circuit, you have to have a good connection and a good ground. If one heart is all corroded and closed off, it can't get the energy from the rest of the circuit. If you are not well grounded to the Earth the signal has no foundation. If a good thought/feeling is sent out on that grid, and resonates to enough healthy heart-minds, real change cannot help but take place. If your chakras are all clean and shiny, and you are grounded to the earth, and open at the top, you are a fine conductor of energy. Focus on blending the energies in your heart chakra, and sending out love all over the grid. I promise it will come back to you. On the internet you can find the "Institute of Heartmath". It is a place to learn much more about this fascinating new science and connect with others that are also connecting with their hearts.

Your conscious mind judges, decides and discerns everything that comes into your energy field. The mind in your heart is connected to all life and vibrates on a slightly higher frequency than your conscious mind. It is from the heart mind that we are all connected to each other, and the oneness of all beings is felt and understood. When these two energies are in unison within you, magic happens. You will begin to live life from a place of grace. Good is attracted to you in every form and contentment and bliss is your normal way of being. The material world is interesting, but holds no great relevance for you. You become a witness to life. Everything is beautiful, and life is fulfilling. It may sound like you are just ignoring life and walking around in lala land, but this is far from the case. Many people use drugs to try and emulate this magnificent state of being, but drugs wear off and there is figuratively 'hell to pay' after that. In true awareness and bliss you are more connected to love, abundance, health, peace, and joy than you can even begin to imagine. Unconditional love is easily offered to everything. Every circumstance has meaning and every soul is glorious. There is no place in you where resentment, dissatisfaction, or disease can reside. This is the mind of the Master.

CHAPTER 21

Hypnosis

Another very good way to change a subconscious program and heal addictions and many other disorders is through hypnosis. A skilled therapist can bypass the critical part of the mind and get right to the damaging hidden belief that is running on autopilot. The trick here is to get to the *real* bottom of a behavior pattern. If someone bites their nails it is fairly easy to get them to quit that behavior by using hypnotic suggestion. The behavior will be replaced by something else that helps the person act out a nervous disorder. Getting to why there is a nervous disorder takes more work. Your subconscious mind knows why you are biting your nails, and it is using nail biting to call out for healing. Your subconscious mind also knows why you are choosing to use an addictive behavior. Once the cause of a damaging condition is found and brought to light, it is much easier to eliminate the destructive behavior. Hypnosis speaks to the subconscious where new seeds of thought can be planted to replace old damaging ones. You can use hypnosis for developing a better self-image, and thus more self-esteem. Self-esteem honors the SoulSelf inside of you. . When you align with your SoulSelf, the gifts of Spirit are cultivated and healing happens. Addictions and pain bodies don't stand a chance when SoulSelf is in charge.

Hypnosis has gotten a bad reputation from stage hypnotists making people act like chickens. Some people are afraid that they will be taken over and made to do things they don't want to do. I assure you that the guy on the stage that is acting like a chicken has a deep desire to have fun or he would not be on the stage to begin with. Usually the real hidden fear is that what you say you wouldn't do, and what you really wouldn't do are two different things. You might be afraid of being found out. Don't worry because the therapist has to take an oath of confidentiality.

You are much more in control under hypnosis than is portrayed on television or in the movies. The stage hypnosis act sets up an expectation about being hypnotized that is not normally accurate. The client expects to be totally "out". In some cases, the somnambulistic state, which is totally 'out', is achieved by a client, but it is not necessary for good results. The more you use hypnosis, the easier it is to go deeper into a hypnotic state. Hypnotherapy is very good for changing unwanted behaviors, but it can do nothing if you resist it. You have to consciously choose to participate and accept the healing.

Rev. Lorana Clark

Using hypnosis with Spiritual Mind Treatment is a very successful tool. Spiritual Mind Treatment is a tool used in my Religious Science Ministry which I will elaborate on in the chapter that follows. Hypnosis really sets the spiritual mind treatment and allows it to take root. Hypnosis also has a branch called metaphysical hypnosis. Taking a metaphysical approach to healing addictions is rewarding. Metaphysical approaches use hypnosis to enhance psychic awareness and seek higher spiritual guidance. When you are working with addictions, nonconventional approaches sometimes work where others fail.

CHAPTER 28

Changing Your MIND

Science of Mind is a philosophy that was founded by Ernest Holmes, He taught the law of attraction in the early part of the 20th century. His first book is entitled *The Science of Mind, published in 1926, Science of Mind is also referred to as New Thought or Religious Science and is not to be confused with Scientology. We have a sister organization called Unity. It was created around the same time by Charles and Myrtle Fillmore. Both Science of

Mind and Unity share their roots from Mary Baker Eddie, who founded Christian Science. Authors such as, Emmit Fox, Emma Curtis Hophins, and Henry David Thoreau are common sources of both Unity and Science of Mind wisdom. The basic tenets of both are;

- God is the source and creator of everything. There is only one source in the Universe and is present in everyone and everything.

- We are Spiritual beings, participating in a human experience.

- The Spirit of God lives within each person; therefore, all people are inherently part of God."

- When we align with the source of life that we are part of, we experience a purposeful life.

- "We create our life experiences through our way of thinking."

- "There is power in Affirmative Prayer or Spiritual Mind Treatment, which we use to re-create our personal reality."

Unity works well as the bridge between Christianity and New Thought. Science of Mind is more of a bridge between New Age and New Thought. This New Thought is actually very old thought. Plato could have been considered a New Thought philosopher. The science of quantum physics is validating what these old philosophers have been teaching for decades, if not centuries. You can find a list of New Thought centers on the internet if you are interested in learning more.

One of the titles I hold is Religious Science Minister. Please don't let the title "minister" lead you down the path of what you've been taught a minister is. Science of Mind is a philosophy more than it is a religion. *I am not going to help you save your soul, but I might be able to help you find it.*

If you have ISSUES: addiction, abandonment, financial difficulties, or abuse, just to name a few, YOU NEED A GOOD BRAIN WASHING. First, get a bowl of water, put in some dish liquid and a little bit of baking soda. Get a bottle brush, wet it well, and stick it in your ear. If it doesn't go all the way through to the other side, that is a good sign. It means that there is hope for you.

To begin to do something about your issues; get a pen and paper and make a list of what you believe is "wrong" with your life. Don't spend too long on this. Use broad statements, leaving the details for *never...* When your list is complete begin to think of what each statement *says* about you. An example might be: my husband is cheating on me-- which might turn into 'I am not worthy of faithfulness'. I need to drink to be able to deal with my job-- might turn into 'I am afraid to face life without a drink'. Of course, there are many possibilities, and each of us has a different story. Be blunt, because you are going to take the soapy water to this anyhow. The "story of you" has gotten dirty, but that can be changed with soap and water. You just have to get in touch with who you are and realize you are not that old story. Getting in touch with your higher power or your SoulSelf gives you the strength to change your story. You need a Spiritual Mind Treatment, and you can give it to yourself. It is better if you find someone to help you, but if you don't have anyone, you can give yourself a tune-up.

Begin by looking at the list of statements about what your issues say about you. Without talking about what you *don't want*, begin making statements that claim what you *do want*. If your husband is cheating on you and that translates to you not being worthy of faithfulness, a statement might be; I am a loving and loyal person who always attracts loving and loyal relationships. A good statement refuting addiction is; I align with the Spiritual being that I am and, I am always free of physical addictions. It won't sound true at first, but it will grow on you if you put your creative power behind it. That is basically what Spiritual Mind Treatment is.

Science of Mind uses Spiritual Mind treatments to bring healing to physical and emotional ailments, and to change the course of events. Unity uses what they call Affirmative prayer, which is basically the same thing. We believe that it truly "is done unto you as you believe", just like the Master Jesus taught us. It is your belief in something that gives it power in your life. A Science of Mind practitioner is trained to make an argument in mind for the object of the treatment. By strongly believing something it puts that belief into the pool of mind where all thoughts go. The strength of the practitioner's belief is so strong that it overrides the client's belief and healing of the circumstance is realized. I am not trying to convince you to join Science of Mind or any other organization. We do not have a credo or a creation story. Our ministers and practitioners are healers and therapists at heart. We teach inclusiveness of all things, because we believe that everything is from one source, which is all God.

We have a phrase in Science of Mind which sums up our basic understanding. It is; "Consciousness is everything". That means that your consciousness creates everything you experience. Another catch phrase is "No matter where you go, there you are" which means that you can't separate yourself from your mental stuff and it follows you wherever you go. If you really understand these phrases you will be able to change your mental picture and shift your life circumstances. Science of Mind teaches that thought is really all there is, and that all healing is first mental healing. You can heal your mental, physical and emotional life by planting new thoughts.

Science of Mind has recently been validated by discoveries on the quantum level. I must apologize for making broad generalizations about this new field of science. I watched the documentary called "What the bleep do we know" and was astounded by how much it confirmed what I have heard from Spiritual teachers over my lifetime. You can get it on Amazon, and I strongly advise you to watch it. I am not a physicist, quantum or otherwise, but I see how the concepts of *mind and matter* fit together. Quantum physics states that *thought is a force in time and space.* Science of Mind teaches that, and it also teaches how to use thought to create events and things in our personal experience. There is a natural law that acts on your attention. As I have said before, if you pay attention to something you feed it. If you feed it with your emotion fueling the fire of thought, effects have to take place. It is a law as constant as the law of gravity. **Emotion plus intent equals manifestation**. Quantum physics has shown us that if you focus your thought on something you can change it at a sub-atomic level. *It is now measurable and provable that a thought is a thing.*

If you constantly worry about people and things, you are sending out your emotion and intent, which will bring what you are worrying about to your door. If you worry excessively about your loved ones, you are *cursing* them. I know that is a strong statement, but it is a deep truth. If you hold worries about them in your mind and put emotion with them, you are attracting your worries to them. Stop worrying is very valuable advice. Some people think that worrying a lot about someone shows how much you love them. Now you see that you can harm them by worrying so much about them. See them like you want them to be- happy, healthy, safe, and secure.

Your words hold much more power than you are generally aware of. What you believe in, you speak of. -- What you speak of consistently, you end up believing. The buzz phrase is "If you name it, you claim it ". When I was first learning Science of Mind, my teacher used to correct me often for saying, "I am trying". Trying is always going to be trying, just as tomorrow never comes. She told me that whenever I make a statement I should start that statement with 'I AM': this will then become my truth. I AM is the name of my Godself and therefore very powerful energy. Words have vibrations and energies given off by the resonance of sound; therefore, I am *"working on"* explaining all this to you. I *intend* to help you learn and grow. I am not "trying" to do anything. *Master Yoda says, "No trying, you are either doing or not doing".*

Your subconscious mind does not know about 'NOT'. In other words it can only accept full ideas. If you say NOT swimming, or swimming it only understands being in water. The subconscious part of your mind is where all the healing happens, and where all the illness starts. The subconscious mind is inductive therefor; **it has no ability to judge**. You can see by this, why it is so important to clean up your subconscious of all its unwanted subprograms. It cannot judge what is good or bad for you, it just knows what it has been told. If you persistently speak negatively or have negative feelings about yourself, sooner or later those emotions translate to the deepest level of your being. If the negativity is constant, your cells will respond with dis-ease.

In Science of Mind we are taught how to speak our word with authority, like Jesus did, to heal ourselves and others. Our words must have our total uncompromised belief in the power behind them, or not much will happen. In a Science of Mind Treatment we start by declaring who we really are. We remind ourselves that we are Godlings: therefore, we have the power of creation within us. Then, we declare that there is a law of mind in the Universe, which is always available, and can be used by all of us. We declare our word to be strong and our conviction and belief in it to be irrefutable. We state clearly and with the authority of Godself, what we know to be the truth of a person, place, or thing. We claim this truth for ourselves, and for whomever we are treating. We then bring in the intense feeling of thankfulness, that what we are choosing is already a fact. Once we have given thanks, we release the energy we have built up and let it go do its work. By the natural law of attraction, our new belief will attract situations and events to bring it into fulfillment.

Jesus said, in Mathew 21 *"Truly I tell you, if you have faith and do not doubt, not only can you do what was done to the fig tree, but also you can say to this mountain, 'Go, throw yourself into the sea,' and it will be done.".* Ernest Holmes took the teachings of Jesus literally and put them to work

Rev. Lorana Clark

Our Science of Mind Logo is a diagram of how we can change our thinking and affect our life circumstances.

The meaning of the Science of Mind Logo

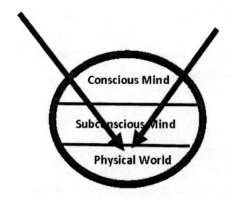

A thought comes in from the **conscious mind** as an idea. If it is a repetitive thought, it gets planted in the **subconscious mind**. Once the subconscious mind makes it a habit, it is planted in the **physical** soil of life. It then grows out of the ground of life as people, places or things that fulfill the original thought. Because of the time delay, you have to plant the seed, and wait for the fruit...

This is how thoughts become things. To change your life you must use your imagination to plant the new idea or thought. That is why our ministry is also called "New Thought".

CHAPTER 29

Pea Soup

In my Science of Mind ministry, I meet many people who want guidance on how to maneuver from one pole to the other in the pecking order of life. They have no idea that they have chosen their circumstances and can change them by choosing different thoughts. It always boils down to being afraid of something that might happen, or mourning something that did. Wanting what you don't have, or having what you don't want. I see people from all walks of life and they are all saying the same things and wanting the same things, just at different levels of existence. Someone from the ghetto usually does not ask how to get out of the ghetto (*although you would think that would be a priority*). They ask how to find the right relationship, job, or health care, that will improve their life as it is.

I have a saying; "*if you swim in pea soup you will turn green*". That means whatever environment you are in will get on you, no matter what you try to do to stop it. If someone does want to get out of the ghetto the first thing they need to do is move, even if they have to walk away. If your life circumstances no longer serve you, nor reflect who you are choosing to become, you *will have to make changes...* Addictive patterns are often but not always the bowl of soup your family and ancestry are swimming in. If you are working with a soul group that has other members in the same circumstances as you, your ability to overcome your situation acts as a guidepost to them. Even if you don't have any idea of the laws of attraction, you will, '*by the choice to change*', set in motion events that will support your new experience. On the other hand, if you would only like to change your circumstances, without the real passion underneath that choice, you will end up back in the ghetto where your consciousness is firmly rooted and you are comfortable. You may change partners or your address, but the overall flavor of life will remain the same.

A child born in poverty can live a life in which they achieve greatness because of it, or live a sorrowful life of pain because of it. I am not necessarily speaking of becoming a movie star or a millionaire, although that is entirely possible. I am speaking of creating a meaningful life, with those you love and being a benefit to your community. The same can be said for choosing a lifetime where you are born in the lap of luxury. It can be very difficult to develop compassion for others, while sitting on a throne that was given to you. Choosing a lifetime where you will be spoiled is just that... spoiling... You must then overcome the soul lessons that come with elitism and entitlement. You can learn compassion by giving it or receiving it. I am not saying that being born wealthy is bad; there are many very wealthy people who give from their heart, and who are very enlightened beings. What I am saying, is that it is just as difficult to learn the lessons of generosity or greed from a position of wealth or lack. Usually people choose to experience life within the context of their social order, somewhere in between joy and suffering.

When a set of mental programs is accepted by a large group of people from a particular country, they begin to run at the subconscious level with anyone who stays in that culture for an extended period of time. . This is the pea soup factor. Even if you isolate yourself from everyone else in your soup bowl you will still turn green because you all have to breathe the same neighborhood air. If the whole country that you are a part of likes polka music, it will grow on you. If your social group hates country music, you will probably grow to dislike it as well. If you were born in that environment, it would not cross your mind that this could be wrong. Prejudice and hatred are kept alive by this principle. The same is true for tolerance and love. If you get together with likeminded people who feel good about themselves, you will begin to grow in strength and self-esteem. The Feel Good energy gets fed and grows. It doesn't matter to mind what you're feeling good about, any more than it matters to a computer what keystroke you use.

In Science of Mind, we call your environment and mental climate, *race consciousness*. Race consciousness is not your ethnicity, it is the climate of thought that you are surrounded by. Said another way, it is the PEA SOUP bowl you are currently swimming in. People in the Orient are thought to have a mindset that values reserve. If you are born in South

America, salsa is your social climate. People from the city might think that country folk are ignorant, or unrefined. They believe it is dangerous in the woods, and bears will eat you. People from the country think the people from the city are snobs and ignorant about the things of nature. To them the urban jungle is much more dangerous than the rural forest, because the urban bears have guns to shoot back.

Wherever you have chosen to be, you will inherit a mindset that goes with that environment. Race consciousness is the predominant thought that the humans of a particular area generate. This is also true about organizations, and large corporations. As an example; China starts the work day with an attitude adjustment that helps put their workers into the consciousness of community and productivity.

If you have chosen a lifetime of difficulty, you will likely gravitate to others with the same issues. The old saying, "misery loves company" is a deep truth, but unfortunately not a productive one. If you are miserable and stay with others that are just as miserable, it is much harder to climb out of that bowl of soup. You identify with the lack, loss, and the "ain't it awful" crowd. You will all talk about how bad it is and how poor, sick, or brokenhearted, you are. This only serves to strengthen your current circumstances. You are *paying* attention, with emotion and agreement from others, to what is wrong in your life. If things got better, you wouldn't have anything to talk about with your friends. If paying the bills becomes, not only the goal, but the prize, then all you will ever get is enough to pay the bills. If you only talk about "the bills" that is all that's going on in your life, and you attract more bills.

On the other side of the coin, once a seeker of wealth and power gains their objective, the lust for power and possessions can turn into greed. When greed takes over, it sooner or later kills the body or consumes the Spirit with the stress of protecting what is yours. It is like Gollum in *"The Lord of the Rings" protecting "MY PRESCIOUS". Power and possessions can become a burden. I know that sounds incorrect to someone that is "just getting by". They say "if only" they had a million dollars they would be happy. It is just like the Page-ites; once you have something valuable, you have to put energy into protecting it. Power can become a big responsibility. Learning that the things of this world are transient, and happiness comes from recognizing yourself as SoulSelf, not the body you inhabit is where you find peace and happiness. Once you understand this you are free to have, or not have, lots of *stuff*, because your stuff no longer defines you or your happiness.

Once you understand what you really want, you can set your powerful creative attention into action and improve your circumstances, no matter what bowl of soup you are swimming in... To change your personal financial situation from poor to lavish, you would have to have placed learning to deal with what lavish means in your primary soul contract. You would have to have the consciousness for wealth, because consciousness is everything. Without the proper consciousness about wealth, your money will not stick around very long. Wealth and comfort are not necessarily the same things. You can certainly go from lack to comfort in life, if you put your mind to it and follow your heart. There is enough "good" to go around. It is your ability to attract good, which brings good to you or keeps it from you. It is your soul contract that determines how that good looks to you and others, because you chose your cultural surroundings before you incarnated. If you live in the Sahara desert, a camel looks pretty darn good. If you live in Venice Italy, it might be a boat. In America, it could be a nice luxury car or a really nice motorcycle. It doesn't have to be about abundance. The same energy can be applied to your relationships or your health issues. Take steps to swim comfortably in the bowl of soup of your choice. If you don't like the soup, you can open another can!

CHAPTER 30

Purses, Princes, and Parking Places

In early Science of Mind classes we are taught a law we call "purses, princes, and parking places" The reason for this is quite simple. Most often a student will be attracted to our teachings because one or all of these areas of their life have become unmanageable. Their money is gone, their relationships are in the tank, they can't get what they want in their career, or even a decent parking place. They are desperate and they want help. They see themselves as victims of circumstance. They want answers and they want the power to change their life experiences. Through the study of your mind, you can indeed find that power. Once you begin to grasp the concept of being made of God-stuff, you can claim the power to change things in your life.

Spiritual Mind Treatment is about claiming your power to heal or create, stating your intent, summoning it into being, and giving thanks that it has happened. Then you release the energy to go do its work. Prayer works exactly the same way, if you are accepting instead of beseeching. Calling yourself a small, insignificant, unworthy sinner before you ask for something and then not expecting to get rewarded until you die, will not get you very far. You become more pitiful than you were to start with. You have to whip up the energy, State it, Claim it, Give Thanks for it, and Let it Be!!

Affirmative Prayer or Spiritual Mind Treatment is not very different from a Witch drawing down her power from the Moon, stating her intent, expecting magic to happen, and then proclaiming; SO MOTE IT BE...An Evangelist minister is making magic happen when he gets his congregation all stirred up and claims the power in the Blood to HEAL! He ends his declaration with thanksgiving; "PRAISE THE LORD"... A prayer group can manifest miracle healing by their belief. Someone in deep despair who has finally surrendered and turns to prayer will find healing. It is not because he is Christian, or Jewish, or Pagan, or any other religion. It is because he is using a natural law that is always there to be used when the mind and heart are focused.

We believe we must search for joy, when the truth is that we must allow joy to be what we are. We believe something must be difficult or it is not valuable and that we must fear the world, and often times the God that created us to be in it. If there is something in your life that you don't like, in fact you hate, you have to **love it** before you can **leave it**. That means you have to accept it and see what it is trying to teach you. You have to be thankful for the lesson, and then you can move on.

The job, the relationship, the addiction, or the circumstance that has you upset can only be changed when you first accept it for what it is. If you claim your circumstances as soul choices, you are no longer the victim of something that you have no power over. If you choose to study math in college, you do not blame the instructor for your choice. If you are not very good at math, perhaps after toughing out a semester you will change your major to history. Life lessons viewed in this way bring empowerment instead of resignation.

Start with something simple, like a traffic jam. This is a very hard concept to grasp at rush hour, while you are in traffic and frustrated. You can change how you're feeling about what you are witnessing, or at least not let it hook your attention in such a way that it sucks you into the fray. It is unreasonable for most of us not to slip into frustration now and then, especially in traffic. The key is to become aware of your frustration, instead of being on auto pilot and allowing it to run through your energy unfettered.

Once you can become aware of your inner state of being, you are able to choose to feel differently about it. That is what being "mindful" means. While in a traffic jam, you can play with the idea of being slowed down to take the time to *chill out*. Having a book on cd is a very nice way to pass the time. Sometimes the delays in life are actually keeping you from being somewhere that you shouldn't be. A missed plane can mean you might be better off staying where you are at, or it could be a chance meeting of someone important to you, before you leave the airport.

It is also important to honor the emotions you are feeling. If you experience a loss it is normal to grieve. Suppressing normal emotions can lead to mental illness.

Remember that surrender and acceptance can bring healing to your circumstances. The stages of mourning after the death of a loved one are natural and should not be avoided. When you suppress and avoid them, they will wait around until your back is turned and sneak up on you when you least expect them. They would have been healed if you had accepted them and worked through the loss when it happened. This is also true for the loss of a relationship. It may well be that you are attracting unhealthy relationships and you need to work on those issues, but you still need to accept the loss of your partner. Losing anything, or anyone, that deeply affected your life will need time to be grieved over. Avoidance patterns revolving around loss often lead to addiction.

It is absolutely true that you can use the tools of attraction to bring specific things or events into your life. Be careful what you ask for because you can get LITERALLY what you are saying you choose. For those who are not really sure what they want, it is best to request concepts like harmonious personal relationships, or comfortable income. It is far easier to leave the particulars to the universe. To literally choose is like going to a China Buffet and only eating steamed shrimp, when there is so much to choose from. Let the Universe decide what harmonious personal relationships will look like. They will be drawn to you by the degree of harmony within you. Be clear on your intent, but don't limit yourself in the process. You must also realize that until you understand the pain body, harmonious relations could be less than wonderful. IF you are still fighting your pain body, being specific might be best. You will have to consider your personal circumstances and do what feels right for you.

Some Science of Mind Ministers teach that you need to be very specific. If you decide to study New Thought in more depth, you can try it both ways and decide what works best for you. I was taught to be very specific when I first started using the law of attraction with Science of Mind. I was in the market for a new relationship. (I had flunked relationship 101 and 202). I listed all the attributes I would like in a partner. I was creating a shopping list. Some of the things on the list were intelligent ++, must have motorcycle, be a Spiritual seeker, and have a good income. I got a biker genius who needed someone to make sure he went to work at his high paying job with the same two shoes on. He was very spiritual and eventually left me to become a Buddhist Monk. BE CAREFUL WHAT YOU ASK FOR!!

In truth, I can see where my Monk husband was very instrumental in my life. I suspect that we had a soul contract. The Archangel Michael teachings found in "Messages from Michael", speak of "task companions". Task companions are people you share your life with for a certain purpose, but they are not meant to stay forever. I believe my monk and I were task companions. I am grateful for our time together. He gave me many opportunities to grow spiritually, and I hope I helped him grow in Spirit as well. Always look for the gifts coming from your relationships and don't dwell on the negative. If you are getting beaten, it would be good to get out of harm's way before you begin your journey into self-discovery. Something within you has attracted this person into your life, but accepting the punishment is never the way to fix things.

Rev. Lorana Clark

Science of Mind Treatment for General Good

Notice that I use the five components of manifestation.

They are; **God is, I am, I choose, I give thanks and I release.**

There is only one source in the universe, one presence, and one power, in and through everything that is. It is within that one source that I think, move and have my being. The one source responds to me with the same creative power that created me. I am a point of energy within *"All that IS"*. As I create with my mind, within the one mind, I set in motion the intention of my thoughts. I declare that within, through and around me there is only peace, harmony and mindfulness. I am a being of light, and I attract positive energy into my life. I project joy, and I accept joy as my truth. I reside in joy and thanksgiving throughout my interesting, fruitful and healthy life. I am so grateful that I can share my creativity and my joy with others wherever I go. I see only the good in all experiences, I am thankful for the good in my life, and I am thankful for the good in everyone's life. I release this word with the full authority of my SoulSelf. My word can only come back to me fulfilled, because that is the Law. I release with gratitude... AND SO IT IS!

CHAPTER 31

Bring in the Computer Geeks

When trying to change your life, it is helpful to equate your subconscious mind with a computer. Perhaps, we got the ideas for the workings of computers from what is really going on in the supercomputer between our ears.

As stated before, deeply held beliefs are always working in your subconscious mind. They have been planted there and are perennial. Until you uproot a subconscious belief or override the program it will just keep on running. In a computer, sub-programs are always running in the background, setting the climate for your computer experience. They keep the hard drive going and the processes happening when they should. Your subconscious mind holds the subprograms of your physical experience. However, little mental viruses can get in there and undermine your life and happiness.

Thoughts create feelings, and it is the feelings that are really fueling the program. You have to change your feelings about yourself. To do that you start with your conscious mind and begin to decide to change old programs. You can replace old damaging thoughts with new healthy intentional thoughts. It seems like a contradiction to say that it is the conscious mind that will heal the subconscious program, but it is true. It seems like we are using what got us into trouble, to get us out of it. Once you name a subconscious program you can begin to set yourself apart from it. You can witness it and fix it, instead of being a pawn to it.

Traditional psychotherapy spends years sorting through your internal junk programs and hopes that you can fix them with the light of awareness. This can and has worked to help many people be happy and well-adjusted individuals. If you don't have the time or money to devote to conventional therapy, you can hire the Cosmic Computer Geek to come fix you up. There are ways that you can fix your computer by overwriting a program that doesn't take all the time and money professional therapy does. It takes a knowledgeable programmer and good virus software. You can learn to be a computer programmer with books and classes. You can learn to be your own mental programmer with books and classes on Science of Mind or any similar school of study. It is the ***do it yourself, handyman healing method.***

Most people who really need a program override can easily see what is going wrong. Their health is bad, their relationships are dysfunctional, or their finances are in a mess or nonexistent. They may be addicted to a substance or an avoidance pattern, masking the deep pain that is created by the subprogram. It doesn't matter what the symptoms are, the computer uses all the same mechanics. As for finding the hidden program causing the malfunction, we can look at the abuse suffered as a child, and see it pretty clearly. It doesn't take a lot of work to understand why an incest victim would have some emotional difficulties that would cause a hard drive malfunction concerning relationships. Physical and mental abuse is also high on the list of suspects to be sure. Ironically, people who had a fairly normal childhood often have a harder time finding the program bug than someone from a dysfunctional family. Buggy programs are somewhere in there, or there would be no problems to solve.

It's not always necessary to know exactly where your negative or destructive beliefs came from. You may have downloaded a virus from your parents, or carried one in from a past life. It could be the country music song that was playing while you were sleeping. One of the worst things you can do to yourself is go to sleep with the TV or radio on. You are in an altered state of awareness while asleep and your critical mind has let down its guard. The morning is not as sweet after a night of crime scene investigation, or perhaps a dose of monsters invading Cleveland, having bombarded your subconscious all night. Violent video games or movies can program your mind toward violence, and then you will attract more of it in your waking life. The choice of what you put into your mind creates the overall climate of your circumstances.

If you want noise to sleep, make it relaxing music or sounds that have no message, like rain or the ocean. I have positive meditations to go to sleep with, and they have improved my outlook nicely. I highly recommend * "The Secret Universal Mind Meditation" by Kelly Howell. As always, it is your choice. It is the old adage of Junk in, Junk out. Good programs in, good programs out. Any programmer knows that sometimes you have to sort through miles of code to find the bug in the program. If there is nothing in your past that explains why you're depressed, it might be that you believe in your subconscious that ♫ *I'm stuck in Folsom prison, and I ain't seen the sunshine since I don't know when, do da do da*♫.

Habits are things done in repetition that have moved into your subconscious and started running as subprograms. You can create a new habit of mind for yourself, and replace junk programs with good ones. When one program contradicts another you might get a freeze up on the computer screen for a bit, but hang in there, the program you are putting in with intent, will reboot your system. You will have a healthier operating system once the repairs are made. Habits become subprograms in 21 days. It takes 45 days to let the subprogram take root.

Using affirmations is one way to change your inner mind and change your life. An affirmation is a statement about yourself that you repeat over and over, such as "I have an abundant supply of money, my bills are all paid, and I have money left over just to have fun". At first they will seem fake or wrong. To declare that you have abundant finances in your life, while staring at a pile of bills and not having any fun, can seem like a big fat ole fib. Claiming abundance is a good idea, but if there is another subprogram in place about worthiness, your money will come and go as quickly. The old subprogram will baulk at first. If you claim abundance, you might first lose your wallet. It is as if the old program is under attack and is shouting, "no…. that can't be so.., we are poor, look NO Wallet"! You will also have to gear your affirmations toward *deserving* abundance and happiness. A good affirmation might be, "I am happy and grateful for all that I have, all that I am, and all that I can share". If you are dealing with an addiction, affirming that you are free from the control of the substance will kick up lots of resistance at first. You can be sure that your mind, body, and spirit will ultimately respond to the new mental image you are creating. HANG IN THERE!!

CHAPTER 32

Health

When talking about the health of your body, and using the computer model, the subprograms in your computer affect the endocrine system in your physical body among many other things. They can also affect the automatic functions such as your heart beat or your immune systems. When something becomes imbalanced in your system you get sick. The doctor will run tests to see what is going on and try to make the needed adjustments. The Doctor can prescribe drugs that replace the lack caused by the negative subprogram. If you were a computer the programmer would nuke the bug, and write new code to override the infected code. Your computer would be back up to speed... That is often the only way the doctor treats your condition, but you are not really just a computer. You will need to change the thought that created the effect of illness before a complete healing can happen. Nuke the program first and seek the underlying cause of the negativity as well.

If you feel weighted down with negative feelings, have no energy, and are depressed, you might need to speed up your system. Your computer programmer will bring new software to install that will speed up, and clean up your system. The name of that software is "you are worth it". The doctor might call it anti-depressants. The programmers name is Mr. Imagination and it is a good idea to have him on speed dial. You might consider repar(ent)ing yourself. You can even get a new *mother*board if you need to. With a new motherboard you can begin to install healthy programs.

Healing the body must begin in the mind and the emotions. Medicine can affect the mechanical body but it cannot really help the emotional body. The belief that a pill works, often does as much good as the pill itself. The pill can correct a chemical imbalance and hopefully, not create more imbalances in the process. There are volumes of data showing a placebo to be as effective as the real medicine. This happens because our minds are stronger than the chemicals in the medicine. Where medicine falls short, is that it does not treat the entire being. It treats the physically manifested body, but not the mental and Spiritual body that attracted the dis-ease to begin with. Chemicals do nothing to address the deeper cause of the imbalance, which ended up becoming a physical condition.

You may ask here about childhood illness and birth defects. Remember when we talked about the pain body, and remember the gift of Spirit, and the sacrifice some souls make in order to teach the rest of us compassion. An example of this is in the bible story where Jesus is asked about a man who was blind from birth. When asked who sinned; the man or his parents, Jesus replied that neither had sinned. Jesus said, "the man is here to show forth the glory of the Lord". *John 9; And as Jesus passed by, he saw a man which was blind from his birth. 2And his disciples asked him, saying, Master, who did sin, this man, or his parents, that he was born blind? 3Jesus answered, Neither hath this man sinned, nor his parents: but that the works of God should be made manifest in him.* I think he was talking about the gift the man was giving others about compassion. This man had also contracted with Jesus to be an example of healing. Jesus then spoke his **word**, with the full authority of his SoulSelf and the man was no longer blind.

You often hear about miraculous healings that happen because of Faith Healers, Reiki healers, Shamans, Ministers, prayer groups and more. The belief in the healer has as much to do with your body deciding to right itself, as medicine does. If you believe in the healer, you believe in the healing. Your body already knows the perfect pattern of health. You turned away from your health through poor mental and physical choices. You have to claim the health that is at the core of your system. If a disease is not written into your life plan, physical healing is possible, no matter what disease it is. When your life plan has death written in at that time, the healing will be a peaceful and pain free crossing.

If you have a motorcycle accident and loose a limb, it's not likely that you will grow it back. Accidents are usually preplanned for some karmic reason. The diseases that can be healed most readily are the ones that we bring on ourselves by constantly bombarding our cells with negative self-talk.

Herbs, and other natural remedies are very helpful, but medicinal products will not be lasting without the underlying change of consciousness that allows health to return. In fact, if medicine heals one set of symptoms, and the underlying cause is not addressed in your emotional body, a different set of symptoms will eventually manifest.

Expect to be healthy and be thankful for your continuing health. There is a great little book called * "You Can Heal Your Life" by Louise Hay. In it there is a list of diseases and the mental equivalents that cause them. It's certainly worth checking to see what your developed ailments tell you about your inner beliefs. There are also affirmations listed to counteract the damaging belief. If you identify with just your body, you could worry about germs and disease attacking you at every turn. If you choose to be happy, all the nice little hormones can be balanced. The immune system flourishes and the brain chemistry is happy. The software is running smoothly, and all is well.

Sometimes it is difficult to find something to be happy about. Get creative, and think of something! A happy immune system automatically kicks out the germs, just like your virus software will not allow a bug to be downloaded onto your hard drive. Simply having a happy thought will not override a lifetime of unhappy thoughts, but it's a start. A positive thought outweighs a negative thought 10 to 1. Happy thoughts have to be consistent and be the habit of your mental state. You can make that happen, not by hoping outer circumstances will change, but by changing your inner circumstances first!! If you aren't overjoyed with life, fake it till you make it.

CHAPTER 33

Relationships

If you constantly go from one destructive and toxic relationship to another, you probably have a bug in your program that tells you about your self-worth. If you come from a long line of women or men that have flunked the relationship class, you will be prone to attract others that are flunking it also. That is just the law of attraction at work. I believe it is through our personal relationships that we grow the most. In the computer model, we are trying to link up an Ethernet system, when we build a set of personal relationships. If one of the computers has a virus, they all can be infected. In a toxic relationship, if one person is acting out with tyranny over others or playing the victim roll, all the others will suffer. On a soul level, everyone chose to be there to learn different lessons from the same circumstances.

Your internal programing attracts you to the ones that victimize or abandon you. I know that is a pretty hard pill to swallow. If you can get past the victim mode, you instantly realize that by changing your inner program, you will stop attracting the same type of relationship. The buzz phrase "you can only change yourself" is true. If you consider yourself to be with a soul mate, but they are abusing you, or addicted to something, the goal for both of you is to overcome this pattern. Staying in a situation of abuse does nothing but further the virus of abuse. If you find the strength to change your pattern, your soul mate then has the opportunity to learn and grow as an individual and change theirs. Accepting abuse does nothing for either party and keeps you both stuck. Remember the Mud…

If your relationship is about sacrifice and you feel like a good and holy person for putting up with unhappiness for decades, I am sorry to tell you that it is the same program of abuse, reacted too differently. The long suffering won't get you a high place in heaven. You will get to come here again, and try to learn that all love starts with self-love. If you are a rescuer you will attract a broken person, bring them home, and try to fix them up. This is a no-win situation. On the one hand, if you succeed in fixing them up they no longer need you. They leave you feeling used and abused. If you are unsuccessful at fixing them up, they are a broken person stinking up your living room, watching your TV, and eating your food. Now you have to figure out a way to get rid of them.

Don Miguel Ruez who is the author of *"The Mastery of Love" said in one of his workshops that, *"Love is the strongest demon in Hell"*. Yikes, that is a powerful statement that seems to contradict itself. He went on to say, "I ask you; where have you sacrificed the most, and when are you the most vulnerable"? What we do in the name of love can be totally self-destructive. What we do from a place of neediness can be even worse. In the land of duality, love has the other side of the coin which is hate. Love and Hate are very close relatives. *The height of love with attachments is the depth that it can hate when those attachments are not fulfilled.*

If you constantly talk poorly about your partner or about relationships in general, you are relationship bashing. This can only attract what you are sending out. Comparing how "bad it is" is a trap that insures that you will only attract bad relationships. Why? Because you expect to! If we allow others to treat us poorly, we are disrespecting the God within us. Many people confuse emotion and passion with love. The divorce courts are full of people that fell out of love when the passion died. Love as I am using the word, is a glorious, peaceful, presence that is caring, non-judgmental, and supportive. Sexual passion fuels the instinctual drive to procreate and is part of the instinctual being that we are en-souling. Sex is beautiful and sacred energy that enhances love, when allowed to be natural. It is our obsession and addiction to sex that creates multitudes of problems. Sexuality revolves around the survival instinct. It is no wonder that the program bugs in relationships appear to be the strongest problems we face.

It might help to realize that very few of nature's creatures mate for life. Perhaps, we are not one of them. There might be fewer bugs to fix if we didn't see the changing of the guard in relationships in such a negative light. The guilt placed on "failed" relationships does not come from God, it comes from political religion. A happy marriage that lasts a lifetime may be a joyful exception, but not the rule. I think that many of us have appointments with more than one soul mate in our lifetime. Soul-mates are not always blissful relationship; in fact they are seldom easy. I hear people say "I wish I could find my soul mate", instead of the guy or gal I have been married to for 40 years. Young souls are still looking for the charming knight, or princess that worships them. Good luck with that! Soul-mates are often the hardest, yet most personally rewarding relationships that you either keep or overcome.

Chapter 34

Wealth

The law of abundance is directly attached to your sense of self-worth. Abundance is always available and there is more than enough for everyone. You have to be willing to receive it. If you have a subprogram running that says you are not worthy, success will pass you by. Even if you have lots of money, you won't be happy with it. You will miss the bus to the interview for the great job, or get robbed, lose your purse or your job. Every time something good comes your way, something bad is there to take it away. You will feel guilty or mean spirited, because of what you have or don't have. For some hidden reason, you got the viral message that you are not good enough, and you must be better, do better, and be smarter, etc. before you can enjoy the good things of life. You may be able to see where you got this program, or it may be a mystery. It is simple arithmetic; if your financial picture is not healthy you have a bug in your program that needs to be deleted.

Before awareness, your belief is that you are what you have. If you believe you are worth nothing you will either have nothing, or get all that you have taken from you. You could also become obsessed with greed, amass vast amounts of wealth, and worry about losing what you have. Sooner or later what you have *has you*. Greed is about an obsessive need for power and control. You are afraid that you won't have enough to survive.

If a person has a healthy consciousness of abundance and their conversation with money is in the triple dollar digits, they will most likely always be in that bowl of soup. If you are a person with a healthy conversation with money, but your conversation with money is only in the double digits, then that is the bowl of soup you will swim in. Each person with a good abundance program is happy in their bowl of soup, and feels like they have plenty.

It all boils down to fear. By treating the cause of the fear we can have a rebirth in abundance. Many people seem driven to succeed and are never satisfied with what they have accomplished. They always seem to have something to prove. It isn't always about feeling that you are not good enough to succeed because your parents tore you down. Sometimes they come from well-meaning parents that always praised them for what they did but added that they could also do better. The hidden message was that they were never quite good enough. There is always a BUT in their self-approval rating. Your self-worth problem may not have come from your parents, there are peer groups, and pain body karma issues that will tell you that you are not worthy.

Once you begin to rewrite the worthy program and the deserving program, financial situations smooth out and you will have what makes you happy. If you have a virus in your wealth subprogram the survival hormones can kick in, and you feel like you are in danger of losing your life. Once the survival or desperation energy gets swirling around you, the law of attraction brings many more things to feel desperate about.

I know people that are so afraid someone will steal from them that they lock everything up all the time. If they step out of the door to get the newspaper, they lock the door behind them. Of course they will attract a thief just to prove themselves right, and every now and then they will lock themself out. They set up the energy of loss and loss comes to them.

There are people that can't get rid of anything. They are called hoarders. They are buried in their stuff for fear of not having enough. To the hoarder, their stuff represents their worth, and their safety. They live in a huge cluttered mess because they are afraid to let go of anything. The rule of thumb is messy outside, messy inside. Locked up outside equals locked up inside. Fear of loss is the common denominator. I knew a person who was a hoarder, and afraid of having his stuff stolen. In a way he has created a checks and balance system. He was always getting things stolen, and then he had room for more stuff.

We teach in Science of Mind that we are to consider ourselves children from wealthy parents, who need never be denied any good thing. The creator of the Universe wishes us to live a joyful life. This is not to set up a "spoiled child" ideal. It is to set up the expectation of abundance. Once the expectation of plenty is planted in your subconscious programming, the law of attraction goes to work to make that your truth. If you want abundance in your life, give things away. Release what no longer serves you. That way you are making room for more. When you are giving, you are given to. Of this I am absolutely positive.

When I suggest that we are creating our circumstances, I often hear, that's nice but; *"The Reality is"* this or that, and *"The world is like that"*. When you hear someone say that you should get in touch with reality, it means you should agree with their reality. These people think that they are pawns to some outside force and they usually live in fear. Most people believe that the reality is "out there" and they are to maneuver in the sea of it. To get someone to understand that there are multiple realities available to them is most difficult. You can watch 3 people walk down the street and be sure that their perceptions of the street will all be different in some way.

CHAPTER 35

The Awakening

I t does not matter whether we are young, mature, or old souls. It is prophesized in various traditions, that it is time for an awakening on this planet. No one knows for certain what the coming age will bring us. Perhaps, we will have a New Earth that is less dense to live on. Perhaps, we will choose to begin anew, as a primitive society on a lush green natural Earth. Possibly, we will give up on the land of duality and know our place in the Stars. I am certain that there are people all over the planet, at this time, which are waking up and realizing that there is more to life than what they formerly believed. Many people are asking questions that a few years ago would not have even crossed their minds. If we could put the media to work spreading empowerment and oneness, we would have a different world very quickly. The need to hide under the bed in addiction would vanish quickly as well. I am sure that there are many souls here who are helping with the process. I choose to be a catalyst for that awakening and you can too.

The internet is a source of many organized and focused meditation groups that help bring peace and harmony to this planet. Meditation by many minds focused on one goal will bring about the intent of the meditators. It is much like a mass Science of Mind treatment. It can also be thought of as purposeful hundred monkey thinking. It is possible that a new way of thinking will spread until it is commonplace to be aware of whom we are and that we are all connected to each other. Once we realize that the climate of our mind is important and makes a difference, we can use our life journey to tip the scales toward peace and enlightenment for all. The awareness that we are all ONE negates the need for duality as a way to distinguish one from another. The illusion of duality will no longer serve us the same way, if at all, and we will know a new truth for a new age.

Balancing the Energy for Earth

In an LBL session, I was transported to a work group of 4 souls. We were "balancing the energies for the Earth". Each of us had one of the four elements, fire, air, earth, and water. I had the element of thought, which is air. My partner across from me had the element of emotion, which is water. The partner to my right had crystals, rocks, and mineral life, which is earth. His partner had trees, plants, and vegetable life, which is fire. There were two males and two females pared up as opposites. We had to collect our energy and cast it into the middle, on the cross hairs of our circle at just the right speed and pressure. When we got it just right a burst of the most beautiful light was created. I was aware that this was not an easy task. Getting the energies coordinated was very difficult. We had to merge with each other perfectly. I was aware that there were four groups of four in each cadre, and there were many cadres positioned all around the Earth. We were on the astral plane not the physical one. I get the sense that I am participating in this, even while I am here having a physical life. It felt like we were attending a *birthing* of something spectacular

The Green Crowd

In another session, I was directing soul energy, and I was "in the green crowd". The soul energy was like a big rushing green river. I was at a fork in the river and it was rushing by me very fast. Souls were choosing which fork they were going to take and I was somehow helping them by directing traffic. It seemed quite chaotic.

What I was made clearly aware of, is that it is **_gigantically_** important that we get our fear in check. If there is going to be some big catastrophic event we will need to have all our positive energy available to us. We can store up food and guns to defend our physical existence, and possibly survive. If I were 40 years old, perhaps I would have the energy to live in a primitive world. I am in my 60's. I would rather not have to tote wood, and carry water again. (did that in the 60's).

The Purple World

In one of my visions, I was on a strange planet with a very green sky and purple water. There was a group of us sitting on a beach. We were concerned because there was an ocean over the dunes from us, and something strange was in it. We had to go fishing for our food, and some of the men were going over the dunes to do so. We were all anxious for their safety. Three beings of light floated in and told me that I was going to be an elder here. I said, "I don't want to be an elder here. I want to go with you"! I want to explore the universe.

I am certain of one thing; either the Earth will quake, the sky will fall, or nothing much will happen at all, but you must choose whether you want to be Obi Wan Kenobi or Darth Vader... Use the Force, and traverse the duality of illusion with grace. Make deposits in the Joy bank instead of the Fear bank. It is not important for you to start a center, or a church, and save the world. Archangel Michael gave me a shout and told me "THE WORLD DOES NOT NEED ANY MORE CHURCHES". You will be "on fire" to share what you have learned and want to shout it from the rooftops. If you choose unity and live in joy, you will spread your energy to your family and friends. You will have read the pages and let your life be a beacon to others. We don't need to save the world outside. We need to save the world from the inside out. **It is time to wake up and graduate with your class**!

The End

Rev. Lorana Clark

Meditation for grounding your energy, and cleaning your Chakra system

Sit in a comfortable position with your feet firmly on the floor. Begin by taking three long slow deep breaths, in through your nose and out through your mouth. Continue to breathe deeply in this way and pay close attention to your breath. As you breathe in, imagine that you are pulling in cleansing life giving energy. As you breathe out, release the tension and negative energy from your body. Focus your energy on your heart. Feel the rhythm of your beating heart, as it takes the oxygen you are supplying it, and transforming it into food for all the cells in your body.

Begin to imagine that you have a root from the base of your spine that goes down into the Earth. Don't worry about your actual physical position because Earth is always connected to you in your imagination. With your <u>out</u> breath imagine that you are sending your energy down that root into the Earth, and making the root grow. With each out breath, imagine you are going down 10ft into the Earth. Notice what the ground feels like. Is it moist or dry as you go deeper? Is it changing the deeper you get? After you have gone 100 ft., stop and experience the Earth Mother as if you were in her womb. Allow the feeling of protection and wellbeing to fill your energy.

After resting there for a short time, begin to rise back up through your root. With every <u>in</u> breath rise 10ft bringing with you the food that the goddess feeds all of her children, equally and without judgment. When you come up to the base of your spine, allow the energy to continue spreading up through your body. As it moves into your root chakra, notice that it is nourishing the color red. Any cloudy or unhappy energy associated with the root chakra is cleansed. As you move the energy up your body, *progress from the red to the orange and nourish it. Move up to the yellow loving and nourishing it. Now move into the Green. Pause at the green, and nourish your heart center thoroughly. After a moment, move up into your throat center and clean the blue energy associated with it. Move into your third eye and clean and open it, The Goddess opens your energy, and you can see the beautiful indigo light. Now allow the Earth energy to burst forth from your being through the crown chakra, and blossom into the light of the sun. Sparkle with the brilliance of a beautiful tree or flower in the early morning dew.*

Accept the energy of the Sun shining down to meet your energy, and allow the energy to flood your being with all the colors of the rainbow. You become a rainbow of vibrant color, happy, healthy, and energized. Bask in the light of the Sun for a moment, and gently allow yourself to come back into everyday consciousness, generating the most wonderful feeling of gratitude for your opportunity to be part of the dance of creation.

Authors and Titles

The Science of Mind; Ernest Holmes

A Course in Miracles; Foundation for Inner Peace

Messages from Michael Series; by Chelsea Quinn Yarbro

The 12th Planet and various other titles; by Zachariah Stitchen

The Five Gospels; by Robert W. Funk

The Journey of Souls; by Michael Newton

A New Earth; by Eckhart Tolle'

The Secret; by Rhonda Byrne

The Mastery of Love; by Don Miguel Ruez

The Secret Universal Mind Meditation; by Kelly Howell

A Story of Soul; by W.H. Church

A.R.E Association of Research and Enlightenment; by Edgar Casey

The Lord of the Rings; by JR Tolken

The Christian Bible

Illustrations

My Credentials

I am an Ordained Religious Science Minister, with a Counseling Practitioners license from Global Religious Science Ministries. I am an Addictions Counselor, and Group Development Facilitator.

It has also been my privilege to serve Spirit for over 40 years as an Accredited Psychic a Spiritual Medium, and a Certified Astrologer. I am honored to have channeled with the White Eagle Group. I am a Vision Weaver in the Icelandic Shamanic Tradition. Spirit led me to become a Reiki Master Healer, a Past Life Regression therapist, Clinical Hypnotherapist, and Behavioral Counselor

Elfish

www.celestialthyme.org

CPSIA information can be obtained at www.ICGtesting.com
Printed in the USA
LVOW11s2240271014

410745LV00007B/22/P